W9-CQV-033

To David,
Live the Life You
with PASSION!
Love

07

LIVE THE LIFE YOU LOVE
WAKE UP...

PRAISE FOR THE BOOK

II

LIVE THE LIFE YOU LOVE

"Wake Up...Live the Life You Love is like a handful of rare rubies, each line a jewel of great value. It reminds me of Steven Allen's magnificent television series, 'Meeting of the Minds.' You will read and reread it and want to buy many copies to send to dear friends. I promise you will love it as I do."

Dottie Walters, author of *Speak and Grow Rich*
President, Walters International Speakers Bureau

"Steven E thinks outside the box about healthy living. In a time like this when we are asking about our economy and our safety, we are searching for internal strength and balance. It starts with us. Steven is there to educate and motivate us to reach further. He has inspired me to reach my goals and I see amazing results. What contagious energy!"

Sherry Benjamins, consulting business owner

III

"In a field where professional standards are still developed, Steven E stands out as a first-rate professional trainer who has helped hundreds live up to their full physical potential."

Thomas C. Furlong, L.A. Times

"The bite sized wisdom contained in Wake Up...will inspire and uplift your spirit."

Mark Victor Hansen,
co-creator of #1 New York Times best-selling series
Chicken Soup for the Soul.

"Wake Up...Live the Life You Love is a roadmap to leadership, success, and personal power."

Brian Tracy,
#1 best-selling author of *Success is a Journey:*
Making Life a Grand Adventure

ALSO BY STEVEN E

1994

Wake Up

An Inspirational Handbook

2001

Wake Up...Live the Life You Love

(1st Edition)

2002

Wake Up...Live the Life You Love

(2nd Edition)

2003

Wake Up...Shape Up...Live the Life You Love

For your free gift, go to: **www.wakeupand.com**

WAKE UP...

WAKE UP...

WAKE UP...

LIVE THE LIFE YOU LOVE

V

By Steven E
&
Lee Beard

Inspirational "How To" stories to bring more
Joy, Love and Prosperity into your life.

WAKE UP... LIVE THE LIFE YOU LOVE

Published by:
Little Seed Publishing, LLC.
P.O. Box 4483
Laguna Beach, CA 92652

COPYRIGHT © 2003 by Global Partnership, LLC

Pre-Press Management by TAE Marketing Consultations
Robert Valentine, Senior Editor; Katie Dunman, Associate Editor
Text Design: Bob McLean.

Cover Illustrations: Stephan T. Benjamins
Photo Credit : Stephan T. Benjamins

Acknowledgement is made for permission to quote copyrighted materials.

Printed in the United States of America.
No part of this book may be used or reproduced in any manner whatsoever
without written permission of the publisher.
For information, contact Little Seed Publishing,
P.O. Box 4483, Laguna Beach, CA 92652, or phone 562-884-0062.

Distributed by Global Partnership, LLC.
Distribution Center: P.O. Box 894, Murray, KY 42071,
Phone: 270-753-5225 SAN:255-4168

Library of Congress Cataloguing-In-Publication Data
ISBN: 0-9644706-4-0
$14.95 USA $24.95 Canada

VI

For your free gift, go to: **www.wakeupand.com**

 DEDICATION

To all those who dreamed, who pursued their dream with
unshakable faith and who now live the life they love, this book is
dedicated with respect and admiration.
We also dedicate this book and all its promise…

To Steven E's Mom
Janis Schmitt
1933-1997

To Lee's Father
Robert S. Beard
1912-1992

To Mark Victor Hansen
Mentor and Friend

&

To John Assaraf
A Teacher and Guide

To Greg S. Reid
A True Giver

LIVE THE LIFE YOU LOVE

VIII

CONTENTS

For your free gift, go to: **www.wakeupand.com**

CONTENTS

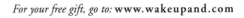

For your free gift, go to: **www.wakeupand.com**

x

CONTENTS

XI

For your free gift, go to: **www.wakeupand.com**

CONTENTS

XII

Congratulations on your commitment to improving the quality of your life! You are not reading this book accidentally. You picked up this book in the hopes that it might inspire you to live a fuller, richer, happier life and we truly believe that you can!

How would you like to be more successful in your career? How would you like to learn how to build and maintain strong relationships? How would you like to live a life you love? We guarantee that, by reading this book and taking the right actions, you will be able to start living a more fulfilling and rewarding life.

This book gives you the resources from mega-best selling authors, success coaches, relationship experts, and other top professionals to make certain you have the tools to create the life you have always desired.

The purpose of this book is to show you how to achieve emotional, mental, and physical balance and to provide motivation and inspiration in all areas of your life. We know that there is a healthier, happier, more successful you that is waiting to wake up! We promise you that this book will help bring it out, if you promise us that you will use the advice in this book to begin living a personally designed life.

Remember, with the right mindset, feelings, and actions, we can shape our destiny. Together, we can live a life we love. Now, let's turn to *page 1* and really get started!

Steven E and Lee Beard

XIII

WAKE UP... LIVE THE LIFE YOU LOVE

XIV

Conceptualizing Your Purpose
Mark Victor Hansen

No one ever succeeds without a clear grasp of purpose. When you look at the lives of the most successful people who ever lived, you can see that they had a definite purpose and they knew it.

Christ's purpose was spiritual and was stated in John 10:10:
*"I am come that you might have life,
and that you might have it more abundantly."*
Walt Disney's purpose: *"To make people happy."*
Andrew Carnegie's purpose: *To manufacture and market steel."*
Mother Teresa's purpose: *"To care for and comfort the poor, sick, and needy all over the world."*

What is your purpose? You cannot find the answer in a book or a class, but wouldn't it be fantastic if you could? The answer can only be found deep inside of you.

How do you find your purpose? My suggestion is meditation or deep, controlled, concentrated thought. Find a quiet place where you won't be disturbed. Relax and tap into your mind, 'way back there in the deepest secret compartment of your mind by asking yourself this question: "If I knew my life's purpose, what would it be?"

Don't just ask it once. Keep asking this question until you get the answer. It may not come on the first day, or even the first week. But it is there, and it will show itself if you earnestly ask. Your constant and sincere question is like a beacon that will draw your purpose to your consciousness and show it to you illuminated clearly.

Meditate on your purpose every morning and every night for 15 minutes until the answer comes to you. Then, be sure to write it down. Don't be surprised if it comes to you during the day while you are exercising, while you're at the grocery store, or taking the dog for a walk. Be open to the answer, no matter when it comes to you.

1

For your free gift, go to: **www.wakeupand.com**

Remember, your purpose is the deepest expression of yourself. In a way, it wants to find you just as much as you want to know your purpose in life.

Let us hear from you,

Mark Victor Hansen
America's Ambassador of Possibility
PO Box 7665, Newport Beach, CA 92658
Co-author, *Chicken Soup for the Soul* series and the *One Minute Millionaire.*
www.markvictorhansen.com

2

LIVE THE LIFE YOU LOVE

Steps
Wendy Schmitt

I want to share what I have discovered that helps me to be free and be true to myself. When I was searching for more from life, I looked inwardly and found something I like to call Spirit--that something that guides each one of us. It's that little voice that will direct us if we just listen.

We all have Spirit, but it usually takes courage to acknowledge it and follow it. Mine told me that it was time to be more. So I took a chance. I let my Spirit guide me. I started to break away from my comfort zone and I found that there was so much more to life.

I met this incredible man whom I believe to be my twin soul. He took me to a new level. It is because of the guidance of my Spirit that I found him and that I live a life surrounded by love. My perfect Other is now my husband, my teacher, my partner in life, and my friend. Steven E has ignited a passion within me and continues to inspire me to realize my dreams and to walk through my fears.

Each of us has a unique path. Take a chance. Follow your inner voice and make your dreams a reality.

I wish you peace, love and happiness on your journey.

Wendy Schmitt
Loving Wife

4

Life With Aloha!
Larry Boren

We read about passion, meditation, goal setting, financial preparation, nutrition, parenthood, health and exercise, peace of mind, loving, personal and physical development, achieving happiness, etc. etc. As a high school health education instructor in my 20's, a real estate agent selling homes, condos, and apartments in my 30's, a real estate broker contributing to the success of over 40 real estate agents in my 40's and now 50's, I find that basic wants and needs have not changed. The decision making process, however, must be faster for more positive experiences and results.

My soon-to-be-a-teenager son, who watches "Happy Days" on TV, recently told me that he thinks we might be happier living in the "slower" 1950s and 60s. Were we? While he did miss some amazing changes in our society, I believe that we can still appreciate the wonders of life and ourselves as much today and, perhaps, more than in yesteryears, especially with the Aloha Spirit I have learned to incorporate into my life.

I built a home in Hanalei Bay, Kauai, in the late 1970s and enjoyed socializing with these true Hawaiians as often as I could get to our "second home" for more than 3 decades. They were able to share their Spirit of Aloha and the beauty of their attitudes as they evolved with the changing times on this charming island that had only one traffic light when I built the home. Change is stressful, and these Hawaiians experienced the stress of dramatic change when the island grew with tourism. At the same time "mainlanders" built thousands of homes to live in this paradise.

The Hurricane Iniki almost leveled the entire island in 1992 and really created major losses of homes, jobs, and income. There was no electricity for over 6 months. It took years for them to

5

recover. I noticed the 1992-93 telephone directory seemed worthless because of all the disconnected numbers as people had to leave the island to survive financially. The remaining people partied in the streets, surfed, watched sunsets, and lived life passionately during these tough recovery times.

Could you do this? Beautiful scenery helps, but they did have a special attitude—an Aloha Attitude. What is that? The word is used as a hello greeting, a goodbye, and also as an affectionate "with love". It also symbolizes a non-aggressive way to live your life in dealing with others—from your true loved ones to anyone on the street. It is a Hawaiian "Golden Rule" that flows like the Hawaiian waterfalls through the island. This life with Aloha even includes a "pass it on" attitude to do a favor for someone with no expectations of a favor in return.

How can we live life with Aloha? This book of contributions has most of the answers. How do we take these positive experiences and successful wise decisions and internalize them into our lives? Well, we go the extra effort to attend these self help seminars/sessions with the best of intentions, yet fail to follow through with the suggested lifestyle changes quickly after the sessions. I still want to improve the life lessons I learned at a seminar about 25 years ago.

So why do I keep going if I know the answers? I guess for the same reasons that keep people going to weight reduction classes, Alcoholic Anonymous, smoking hypnosis. They offer reinforcement and encouragement to keep us motivated. Maybe this Aloha love and spirit theory will make one more contribution in a positive direction for you. Find it. Find the sunsets, the people who care for you—the golden rule people. Become someone who takes time to enjoy the journey instead of only the destination. Be someone who will smell the plumeria, ginger, and pikaki, (OK: roses if the others are not available); someone who will find the Aloha joys of work,

LIVE THE LIFE YOU LOVE

play, hobbies, and loved ones. These words of advice, plus my favorite 3 sayings to my son are my hopeful policies that all will value: 1) Your body is a temple.

2) We need all the friends we can get.

3) Make wise decisions—

think it through before—and do the right thing.

Larry Boren, Broker
L B Brokerage, Inc.
(562) 708-9878
boren@lbbrokerage.com

7

WAKE UP... LIVE THE LIFE YOU LOVE

8

For your free gift, go to: **www.wakeupand.com**

Dreams Can Really Come True! Even in Japan.
Yasuyuki Goto

For 13 years, I was a corporate worker, known as a "Salaryman" in Japanese. My day began at 5 a.m. with a three-hour commute to the office each way to the office. My family was asleep when I left for work and asleep when I returned home. My dog was my only company at home during the weekdays. I hated my life.

I knew that something had to change but I didn't know where to start until I learned through a couple of mentors about how successful businesses in the United States could be. They taught me about direct response marketing and virtual marketing and how utilizing the power of the Internet could make me successful. I could do it too! After two years, I was a consultant teaching how to market a business over the Internet to over 1,000 Japanese clients, with an income that was 5 times larger than my original salary. My first co-authored book, an instant hit, has already sold 250,000 copies in Japan. I now drive a Mercedes, but not to commute. And, I am free to eat lunch with my family on any given weekday. What a difference!

I am so thankful to have learned these successful hints in the United States. Once my own business was established, I decided that I wanted to share the secrets of my success so I launched a new business in Japan teaching what I learned and continue to learn in the United States. Due to a prolonged recession, many Japanese people are seeking to start their own businesses, either out of necessity, or simply to get out of that rat race in which I used to run every day.

I am glad that, by helping my Japanese friends, I am able to express my gratitude to my American friends, the enlightened millionaires that I now associate with on a first name basis. Now both my American and my Japanese friends recognize me as that bridge

9

For your free gift, go to: **www.wakeupand.com**

between the two cultures, uniting people who are aiming for the same goal; to wake up and live the life that you love.

Thank you, America, and thank you my good American friends. I love you. *God bless you.*

Yasuyuki Goto
American Contact Office
Las Vegas Millionaires, Inc.
3157 N. Rainbow Blvd. Ste. 181,
Las Vegas, NV89108
702-279-1712
successjapan@dialogjapan.com
www.yazgoto.com

10

Who Says You Can't Be Wealthy
Richard M. Krawczyk, Ph.D.

The voices: you hear them every day, don't you? Maybe they start chattering while you're driving to work. Or maybe it's when you pull those bills out of the mailbox. Are they especially loud on April 15th of every year? Or maybe it's when you're trying to sleep – and can't. I know you hear the voices; if you didn't, you wouldn't have purchased this book.

I used to hear them too, from skeptical clients, financial planners, and brokers, to accountants, lawyers and bankers. If you pay attention, you will hear echoes of these voices everywhere – in the media, the educational system, the rhetoric of politicians, conversations with family or friends, or maybe even yourself.

"Get real!" say those voices. *"You'll never, ever, become wealthy."*

My response is, *"Oh yeah? Who says?"*

11

Most people don't know how easy it is to make money and create wealth. How many immigrant families do you know who came to America with nothing and became millionaires?

If millions of people all over the world are living the good life, why can't you? Don't be like those who will wait their whole lives and then look back and say, "I wish I had tried." Ninety percent of winning is just getting excited! Somehow, from the time we're kids to the time we become adults, we forget how to dream and how to get excited!

The fact remains that many people are one paycheck away from disaster. That's a terrifying feeling. We live in a free country and yet, many of us are like slaves at our jobs. And then one day...*BOOM!* What happens if you lose that job and lose that income? With all your expenses, you might panic. Then what? You need to take control of your finances now! The only person who's stopping you from controlling your life and succeeding is you!

For your free gift, go to: **www.wakeupand.com**

LIVE THE LIFE YOU LOVE

I've spent over 20 years of my life studying the lives of many millionaires. Do you know what they all have in common? They don't just talk about it; they don't put it off until tomorrow. They take *ACTION* and just do it.

There is no secret to becoming wealthy, but there is a formula. Ask any of the subscribers of my free newsletter at

FinancialFitnessTips.com.

I feel blessed that I've had the opportunity to help people from all walks of life with my wealth building strategies. And the first step is to stop listening to the voices. Talk back, and take action! *To Your Success,*

Richard M. Krawczyk, Ph.D
Author and Lecturer
Author of *Financial Aerobics, Credit Aerobics*
As well as other books and home study courses
Publisher of *www.FinancialFitnessTips.com*

2 Wrecks, 2 Lessons in Love
Stacey Smartt

Life is much bigger than any one of us—if we let it be. When I was 12 years old my destiny changed. My dad's car was violently rear-ended at a stop light by a teenager with little insurance. The accident left my father disabled and in tremendous pain. My dad's inability to work was a devastating financial blow. Thankfully he had always saved as much money as possible and my mom, a school teacher, took on exhausting extra jobs to make ends meet.

I graduated from college with a BS in chemical engineering, but that wasn't my true interest. Wanting to be financially secure, my fears drove me away from working in a job that would pay less – even if I would enjoy it more.

Fast forward to Friday, December 27th, 2002. I was 28 years old, traveling to visit my boyfriend for my remaining Christmas vacation. As I stopped for a traffic jam, I looked in my rear-view mirror to find a work truck barreling towards me. I walked away from the accident, but the wreck left me with lasting back pain and discomfort.

That entire week I was frustrated that this one incident had caused so much pain and had consumed so much of my time. Like a curtain that lifted, I realized all the energy and time in life that I was investing without truly experiencing fulfillment. I deeply comprehended that we can never ask for the gift of time back. The wreck symbolized the ending of my old life and the birth of my niece the following week represented the start of a new beginning.

I immediately worked to unlock the chains holding me back. I learned how to overcome a life-long struggle with emotional eating and I strengthened my relationship with God. While the extra weight melted away, my stresses faded, I gained energy, acquired peace, and realized my purpose. Now, my passion is teaching oth-

13

ers how to do the same. I realized that significance only comes when you contribute your gifts to the world. Each of us has a song to sing and together, we are a symphony.

My dad's wreck taught me about the love of God and that of my family. My wreck taught me to love life enough to finally live it with no regrets. Nothing can take that away from me. In the past my fears scared me… *now my dreams release me.*

Stacey Smartt
423-432-2195
Slsmartt@earthlink.net

14

A Father's Love
Dr. Gilles Lamarche

Love can be defined in so many ways. How do you define a father's love when a marriage fails and three small children are present? What decision can a father make that will positively impact his life and that of each child? In 1988 God gave me that opportunity; an opportunity to choose to live a single man or as a father; to be a man of purpose or a wavering man. I am grateful that I chose to be a father and a man of purpose. My purpose was simple and my pledge was written: "I hereby pledge my life to my greatest expression of love and service for the benefit of all human-ity." My children were at the forefront of this pledge and became the driving force for my entire life. My purpose was to show them love and commitment and have them learn by observation; to teach them a strategy that would help them discover their full potentials without missing what the traditional family might have provided.

15

Fifteen years later I look at each child, now young adults, hav-ing graduated from high school and now discovering their passions as they pursue post secondary education. Every day I am honored to receive their emails and phone calls, and to discover that they are making wise decisions, and achieving not only from their heads, but also from their hearts. They are able to express their love of life, family, friendships and community.

Children, the life and breath of most parents, have so much to give our society. So often those who hope to love them most sup-press the gifts they have. The love of a parent is defined by how you help your child liberate the spirit; how you empower them to truly be the people they can be and that they want to be. It is not our job to stop our children from trying and developing their skills, to rob them of life's experiences. Our love strategy must be to allow them to spread their fragile wings, feed their passion and

For your free gift, go to: **www.wakeupand.com**

their talents, and embrace the lessons and differences they bring to our lives.

I am grateful for the love that I have had the opportunity to share with my children, Jason, Alanna and Christopher, and for the love that they share with me daily. A love based on mutual respect and support is love that truly lasts forever. For the opportunity to discover and experience the existence and depth of such love, I am eternally grateful to God and my children. Thank you for being the most wonderful supporting children a father could have. You are, individually and collectively, "the apple of my eye."

To you, our readers, I wish such a discovery and experience.

Dr.Gilles Lamarche
www.gilleslamarche.com
gilles@gilleslamarche.com

16

What Does Success Mean to You?
Keith Smith

What does success mean to you? The first step in living a ful-filled life is to ask yourself "What do I want from life?" As simple as this sounds, most people never take the time to set goals and create a plan to achieve them. So they live life on someone else's terms. In order to live the life you want, you must have clear focus and determination. Have you ever heard someone say "I just need to find myself?" This is a sign of a confused life.

The truth is that we can never find ourselves, we must create ourselves. Decide what kind of person you want to become, then do whatever it takes to become that person. If you don't know what you are looking for, then how will you know when you find it? If you don't know where you are going, then how will you know when you get there? You can create the life you want if you will just decide what it is that you want.

So I ask again, "What does success mean to you?" Keep in mind there is spiritual success, emotional success, mental success, physical success, and financial success. Come up with a definition for success in each of these areas. Some may say that they would be a financial success if they made $100,000 a year. For others, it may be $1,000,000 a year or more. You have to decide what suc-cess means to you. What does it mean to be spiritually successful? What would it take to be emotionally or mentally successful? How much would you have to weigh and how would you have to feel to be physically successful?

After you decide what success means to you, GO FOR IT! Just remember that success is a journey not a destination. After you have achieved some of your goals or when you can see that they are going to come to pass, then dream bigger dreams. You will be as successful as you choose to be. You will be as happy as you choose to be. Life is a choice.

Choose to live the life you want.

Keith Cameron Smith
Kcs@cfl.rr.com

For your free gift, go to: **www.wakeupand.com**

17

18

Purpose in Life
Steven E

We all have a purpose in life. You have a unique talent and personality that nobody else has. Think of something you love to do and figure out how to make a living doing it. When your life is in working order, your whole existence is so much easier and fun.

If you are currently in a job you don't like, take time to work on the things you enjoy and set a timetable for making a change. Be patient with yourself.

If you do not know what your purpose is, sit quietly and go within; ask for the answer, because all the answers are within you.

Think of the things you like to do that brighten your day and make you smile – things you would do without payment; things you would do for enjoyment alone. Finding your purpose in life is recognizing that you can start being "on purpose" in this moment, because being "on purpose" is about loving unconditionally and serving others. Start NOW to follow your interest, even if you know that your career or life situations will have to change.

I am urging you to do it; don't give up on your vision. We only live once, so do what you love. Find your purpose in life and work with a smile. You have a gift to share with the world; don't be selfish. Share your purpose and your gifts. The world deserves it, and so do you.

Focus your thoughts and intentions on loving and serving others. Learn to make giving more important than receiving because giving is in alignment with your purpose. No one has to tell you when you are "on purpose." When you find your passion in life and move forward with an unstoppable drive, you no long question the meaning of your life. Everything you do is synchronized with your higher self. You fulfill people and feel fulfilled from your actions.

When we are born into this world, we arrive empty-handed.

19

We can't take any material items with us when we go, either. The message of life is to GIVE. Learn to give unconditionally and *live a life that you love.*

Steven E
Creator of the *Wake Up...Live the Life You Love series*
www.wakeupcoauthors.com
www.businessolympians.com
www.stevene.com
562-884-0062

Living the Life You've Dreamed
Dr. Jeff Hockings

"What if you're not smart enough to be a doctor?"

When I was 19, that was the question my father asked me when I told him I wanted to go to Chiropractic College. Not a very encouraging question, especially since I had always gotten great grades, played many sports, rarely got in trouble and was overall a really great kid.

As I processed the question, I tried to figure out why my father would ask such a question. At the time, all I could think of was that he didn't think I was smart enough. I became angry and the only thing I could say to him was, "I will become a Chiropractor!" Then I got up and left the room and started taking the action steps necessary to follow my dream.

That conversation happened 20 years ago. Since then I have:

✦ Graduated from the largest Chiropractic College in the world.

✦ Married the love of my life and share a beautiful daughter.

✦ Started one practice from scratch and built it into the largest practice in my area and sold it for over a half million dollars.

✦ Started a second practice from scratch and within 2 years sold it for over a half million dollars.

✦ Bought a third practice and sold it a year later for over a hundred thousand dollar profit.

✦ Created an Infomercial System that I sold to Chiropractors, teaching them how to created incredible, 30-minute Infomercials.

✦ Started my own Chiropractic Consulting company.

During 1998, we had a temporary business crisis that almost made us declare bankruptcy. We had to fire 4 staff, went 4 months behind on our mortgage for our dream home and went into debt for over $350,000 in five months. That was the most crushing stress and pressure we have ever had to go through. We almost lost everything.

We came through that crisis and made a decision that we would never be dependent on one source of income ever again. That led me to arrange our Chiropractic offices in a way that they would be sellable. I sold our last office in May of 2003.

Since then (it is October 2003 now), I have attended John Childers Speakers Training, Mark Victor Hanson's Mega Speakers program, Tom Antion's Internet retreat and been trained by Janet Switzer. During those six months I have written or co-written six books, developed multiple websites, speak publicly, and am on my way to financial freedom. With my all-star team of mentors, how can I fail?

Throughout my journey, I realized that my father wasn't doubting my ability to become a doctor, he was wanting to make sure I had a back up plan. He unknowingly set me on a path of unstoppable determination that is part of my being today.

Dr. Jeff Hockings
President/C.E.O.
First Class Marriage
1-800-914-5547
www.FirstClassMarriage.com
drjeffhockings@hotmail.com

22

Planning to Succeed
Dr. Pierre Dalcourt

I have just confirmed the flight tickets for my family's next adventure vacation.

How exciting!

I spent a significant amount of time researching locations, visiting the travel agent, and searching the Internet for restaurants, hotels, and activities that suit our family's needs and budget. Now we can prepare with confidence. Everything is scheduled and we even have a contingency plan!

Though planning vacations is an exciting experience, repeating this process for our annual trip always reminds me of how people take more time to plan a family trip than they do to plan their health and their lives.

Imagine getting on a plane and hearing the pilot address the passengers with the following:

"Ok, does anyone know where we are going? I guess it doesn't matter. We can just take off and go up for a while until you are tired of that. Then, we will turn right, then left for a bit. If that doesn't work, we will start going down. Hopefully there will be a landing strip close by and we will have enough fuel." Without hesitation you would get off that plane if the pilot had no strategy or plan for the trip.

As ridiculous as that scenario may seem, most of us are "flying blind" when it comes to our life and our health. Why would anyone like your family, friends, or associates follow you if you do not have a game plan for your life? If you were flying a plane, would any of them want to ride on it?

Having a plan is necessary for a successful, fulfilling life. So make an effort to commit to writing down all of your lifetime goals. Then, write your short-term goals for the next month, three months and then the next year. Do you have a clear vision of

23

where you will be in one, five, and ten years from now? Picture what you look like, what you are doing, how you are dressed, how you feel and be precise.

What you think and write today may be different six months from now. So be adaptable. Change is inevitable but essential for survival. The obstacles you will face are not made to discourage you from achieving your goals; they are simply an opportunity to sharpen your skills and strengths, your courage and endurance, your ability and confidence.

Remember--- having no plan is a plan to fail!
Instead...PLAN TO SUCCEED.

Dr. Pierre P. Dalcourt, D.C., D.AC.
1425 Front Street
Hearst, Ontario, Canada P0L 1N0
(705) 362-4425
dr_dalcourt@hotmail.com
www.drpierredalcourt.com

24

When You Do What You Love, and Love What You Do, You'll Have Success Your Whole Life Through
Greg S. Reid

While speaking at a San Diego university recently, I was fortunate that I was not asked to leave the stage. You see, I chose to share with the students in my audience some frightening statistics. I announced that, while many would receive their degrees, few, *very few*, would end up pursuing careers in their chosen field. At this point, the faculty began giving me dirty looks.

I went on to say that, while most students were there to pursue a dream, the dream they were chasing was not their own. Many students enter college to live up to the expectations of family, friends, and society. They've been told they should become an accountant, lawyer, doctor or teacher because of the great future and financial gain. In trying to do what others think they should do rather than following their individual passions, they rarely continue along the same path once they leave campus.

25

Instead, I painted a different sort of picture. Using an off-the-wall example to illustrate my point, I asked each of them to imagine that he or she really wanted to become a banjo player. I said, "What if you took the same period of time and energy pursuing that dream, your dream, your passion? What if you began as an apprentice at a banjo shop, and then worked hard to learn everything about banjos? After four to six years, the same time you would have spent earning a degree that you would not use anyway, you would instead have become an authority on banjos. A real banjo aficionado. Know why?

"Because you'd be following your passion," I continued. "You would become captivated by the topic, and the pursuit of this goal would no longer feel like work, as much as it would be a part of who you are. Staying up late reading and learning everything there is to know about banjos, listening to old songs and then creating new ones would not be a chore; it would become your joy, because you'd be doing what you love."

Now here's the best part. There will always be a call for authorities in any area. So no matter if your pursuit is toward playing the banjo, inventing new ice cream flavors, or discovering the latest medical breakthroughs, there will always be a demand for your services, thus creating success in your chosen field of endeavor.

This is where true happiness and fulfillment comes in: getting paid to do what you enjoy most while living the life you love. Because . . .

When you do what you love, and love what you do, you'll have success your whole life through!

Greg S. Reid
GregReid@AlwaysGood.com
www.AlwaysGood.com

26

Not Bullet-Proof
John Assaraf

I have been blessed: at an early age I learned the value of my health. Plenty of people spend two or three decades believing they are "ten feet tall and bullet-proof," but at the age of 17, I was introduced to reality in a major car accident.

For several months I had no choices concerning my physical condition. Then I started an intensive rehab program. Up until that point, my dream, like that of many other kids, was to play professional basketball. The dream still lingered when, at 21, I was diagnosed with ulcerative colitis. I was absorbing 25 pills a day, including cortisone enemas to help with the severe pain and discomfort of that disease.

It doesn't sound like the story of someone who is "blessed," does it? Yet, it is true, and the reason is simple. Long before it was too late and long before I could develop poor habits, I was shown beyond any doubt that God only gave me one body to hang around in. My job is to keep it in the best operating condition that I can. That includes both the physical and mental elements of the self.

I made that discovery when I was young enough to understand that my body is breakable. I decided that I would not be unable to enjoy the quality of my life due to my abuse of this miracle called body. As I got older I also became aware of the spiritual side of my being. I learned how meditation and calmness allow me to be at peace.

So, today, my regimen includes a daily meditation to connect with the source that created me, along with a workout to keep this body in high gear. I play life to the fullest, and I want this vehicle to last as long as it can. My responsibility is to learn as much as I can about the latest and best practices to make this happen. Prioritizing my physical and mental well being above work and

27

social concerns allows me to take care of me first.

Is that selfish? I think not, for my belief is that everything we do is done better if we do our best.

John Assaraf
Entrepreneur and Author:
The Street Kid's Guide to Having it All
www.thestreetkid.com
john@thestreetkid.com
858-759-9527

28

WAKE UP... LIVE THE LIFE YOU LOVE

From a Small Foreign Village to the Top of Amazon.com
Joel Christopher

I grew up in a beautiful but poor island country. In my village, I was the son of the only doctor, and was blessed with a caring family and an excellent education. I wanted to help, but being young, I wasn't sure how.

When I was 18 years old, I discovered that my father had quietly been funding the education of needy children for years. Only when a local businessman wanted to express his deep gratitude to my father, did I find out the truth. That experience helped me to realize how I could be of service to my village.

I completed my education and came to the United States to make my fortune. Fueled by my burning desire to help those children, I developed a successful physical therapy practice. Knowing this was not going to put me where I wanted to be, I discovered Internet marketing. I was able to successfully find my niche in teaching others how to build online email lists. There were setbacks and failures, but I held onto my dream with tenacity.

My 36th birthday was a cause for great celebration. Not only had I sent 11 children to school, but that day I released my first book on Amazon.com, *Mining Online Gold with an Offline Shovel* co-authored with George McKenzie. Within 13 hours of its release, the book soared to #2 on the best-seller list—topped only by the newest Harry Potter release. I announced the profits from the sales would be put into an educational trust fund for the needy kids from my village.

This was the fulfillment of a dream! I knew that I would reach my goal, but I was surprised by the way heaven and earth moved to help me. The goal created a momentum that continued to build with time. More and more serendipitous events were occurring around me. Why? Because when you give, you always get back more in return.

29

Less than two months after this momentous day, my father passed away unexpectedly. I never even had a chance to show him the book that was dedicated to him. Yet, when I look into the eyes of the young students I was able to help, I see so much joy and hope, and that eases the ache in my heart left by my father's passing. I feel so humbled to be carrying on the work of such a great man.

Joel Christopher
Co-author: *Mining Online Gold with an Offline Shovel*
www.masterlistbuilder.com
joel@successaccess.com

30

From Madness to Miracles
Pamela Harper

I left the rigors of working as a psychiatric nurse in traditional Western medicine, the frustrations of chronic pain, and the torment of drug addiction in order to reap the blessings of living a life that I control.

Nearly three years ago I made a decision to trust God to lead me past my worries and fears. My life immediately changed. I was directed to receive training as a clinical hypnotherapist where I uncovered my dysfunctional core beliefs.

Through the daily use of self-hypnosis, meditation and prayer, I not only get to witness miracles in my professional practice but also in my own life. Everyday, I expect to attract opportunities for health, wealth, and contentment. I live in the energy of solutions and refuse to engage in problems.

My relationships are fulfilling and nurturing because of my involvement with my higher self. Serendipity is common place. I ask for and receive abundance in the same breath. I am blessed with a Wellness Center where, along with my partner and physician, Dr Carol Barnes, we help heal people from the inside out. For two formerly disillusioned health professionals, life doesn't get any better than this.

I am grateful for my soul's journey, which included crawling around on the floor looking for misplaced drug particles in the carpet, suffering from chronic pain and mental breakdown. Even though parts were difficult, without them my life might not have evolved into the one I desire.

By taking control of my miserable existence and turning my thoughts around, I have successfully attracted physical health, mental and spiritual wellbeing. My grandfather told me that all I had to do was persevere and eventually life would fall into my grateful lap. He was right and I am now living a very rewarding and fulfilling life.

Pamela Harper, RN
Certified Addiction Counselor and Certified Clinical Hypnotherapist.
Writer, Lecturer, Media Personality
Family and Holistic Health, San Clemente, CA.
Pamelaharper@permanentchanges.com

32

The Life Bed
Mary Andrews

I love to listen to the stories of senior citizens. How beautiful it is to hear the peaceful words of a person reflecting on life with pride and satisfaction! For most of them, the important things are obvious and they almost boast of having passed some sort of test, cracking a code or finding buried treasure.

Conversely, how painful it is to hear the words of someone nearing death who is looking back on life with regret? The list of "should haves" and "shouldn't haves" is long, and the frustration of being unable to go back is unbearable. I am not referring to minor mistakes like arbitrarily yelling at our kids or working the weekend when we should have stayed home.

I'm referring to a deep, stabbing regret of a kind you have when, on your deathbed, you wish you could rewrite history. The clear vision comes too late, and the best you can hope for is forgiveness - forgiveness from yourself, from the people you've hurt, and forgiveness from God for wasting your life and not fulfilling your mission.

The wonderful news is that we don't have to wait to be on our deathbeds to get that clear vision! When we go to sleep, instead of thinking about the company's budget report, or the new diamond ring we want, we can close our eyes, take a deep breath, and reflect. Is the daily grind of our busy lives on track with where we want to go?

Every choice we make, including the questions we ask,
leads to what our lives become.

What do I want my life to be? What unique gift (and we ALL have one) did God give me? Am I using it? Or am I doing what other people think I should be doing?

Only when we are on our deathbed is it too late to change course. *Why not lie on your Life Bed?* Your joy and satisfaction will guide you. You'll know your purpose because it is something that

33

brings fulfillment to you, but also helps others.

I have so much to be thankful for. The "attitude of gratitude" puts everything in perspective. When I woke up last year after surgery for colon cancer, I was thankful that I wasn't lying on my deathbed, filled with regret, but instead on my life bed, filled with hope. I made the choice to take responsibility for my illness - not in a way that burdens me with guilt, but in an empowering way that asks, "How can I help my body heal and prevent this problem in the future?" Now that I've looked death in the face, I can turn to life and ask, "Why am I here? What unfinished business do I have a second chance to fulfill?"

Life is not meant to be merely endured and survived. We were put here to discover our gifts and to use them. The world needs your gift. Good luck finding it.

Mary Andrews
Marper12@aol.com

34

How One Book Changed My Life
Gino DelCiancio

For seven years I have owned my dream business, Classic Video Productions. I love to spend my working hours taping, editing, and producing videos of special events such as weddings, anniversaries, birthday parties—even corporate videos and seminars. My job is very fulfilling, very flexible, and something I see more as a hobby than as work.

A typical week for me is far from typical for most of corporate America. The work week begins on Saturday, not Monday, and consists of taping an event followed by a week of creative editing. Taping is the most enjoyable part of the process, exposing me to a variety of people, places, and events that I otherwise might never have seen. It is a privilege to capture people laughing, telling stories, and having a great time. This scene was far from what I experienced before I began my own business.

I worked as an assembly line worker for a major automaker. My day began at 4:30 a.m. with an hour-long drive to get to work. Once there, I spent the day doing monotonous, boring work before coming home and crashing on the couch. I did not feel important, respected, or valued. I felt that my worth was based on how many parts I could put on the cars. I was a number. I could be replaced.

One day, while listening to a speaker, I heard about a book called "Think and Grow Rich" by Napoleon Hill. It captured my interest, so I decided to purchase it. After all, what did I have to lose?

It was the best purchase I ever made. The book motivated me to leave my JOB (Hill calls it "Just Over Broke") and taught me that "what the mind can conceive and believe, it can achieve." Never before had I heard that. Never before had I believed that.

As a factory worker, I remember thinking "This is not what I

35

want. This is not my dream life. This is a nightmare." I felt my life slipping away with nothing to show for it except a menial paycheck. But life is different now, thanks to Hill's book. Today I am happier, healthier, and am able to spend more quality time with my family while working a job I love.

If I could give you any advice, it would be to follow your dream. Do what you love to do and find a way for people to pay you. We are all gifted in some way; the key is to find your gift and share it with the world and the world will pay you back handsomely. In the words of Mark Twain, "make your vocation your vacation." Believe in yourself and go for it. *God Bless.*

Gino DelCiancio
Classic Video Productions
Classicvideo@sympatico.ca

36

Open Window, Open Heart
The Healing Art of Listening
Jesse Dean

For years I excelled at a job that I did not like and for years it filled me with doubt and fear, the fear that I was letting my life slip away without expressing my true talents. Driven by an uncontrollable need for approval and security, I did my best to contribute to the welfare of all those around me. Although I earned lots of money to support my family and spiritual community, I was sacrificing my true heart's desire. Over time I became frustrated, poisoned with grief and self-condemnation, feeling my spirit weaken, consumed by my angry obsession with my worldly fumbles and failures. No matter how much I earned it was never enough to allow me to stop and savor the fragrant flowers in my life. In dire straits, my health and business collapsed. The ensuing loss of confidence nearly destroyed my marriage as well.

37

I did not know then that my life's tragedies would later become a strong foundation on which I now offer hope and guidance to other troubled souls. Through my trials, I have discovered that there are healing words and sounds all around us if we will open our hearts and listen in the silent golden light emanating from within. All it takes is a sincere desire to let go and release our negative self-talk while humbly asking for help.

During one particularly dark period during my failure, I found myself mournfully comparing myself to the accomplishments of others and running myself down with negative self-talk. At that time, a close friend introduced me to the practice of chanting the short Buddhist phrase, "Nam Myo Ho Ren Gay Kyo." He showed me how to repeat these six simple sounds over and over again without my understanding their meaning. Within minutes, my chanting released the death grip of negative thinking that was grid locking my mind. I felt a refreshing, life-affirming energy flowing through me which saved me from my brooding contemplations of suicide.

For your free gift, go to: **www.wakeupand.com**

LIVE THE LIFE YOU LOVE

For the 18 years following that experience, I have used the practice of chanting daily to revitalize my spirit. I chant to tap my inner strength and wisdom, trading my negative self-talk for positive affirmations which spontaneously fill my mind with pictures of the good that I desire. Each day I am renewed from within, attracting to myself positive ideas, resources and people necessary to help me expand my awareness and capabilities to achieve victory after victory.

Now, I wake up each day and build the life I love. I work as a professional musician and public speaker offering joy and guidance to others seeking to realize their true potential. I serve as president of my own production company and direct my own private foundation. I focus my efforts to develop relationships that strengthen the light of hope around the world.

I offer my sincere gratitude to my many friends and teachers around the world who have supported my Buddhist practice over the years. To demonstrate my gratitude, I actively support the SGI-USA (see SGI-USA.org) in my community helping to make the powerful healing practice of chanting, "Nam Myo Ho Ren Gay Kyo," available to all, seeking to *wake up and live the life they love.*

Jesse Dean
Jessedeanow@earthlink.net
www.thejessedean.com

Something Beautiful
The Heavens Are Crying
Ryan Marr

As long as I can remember I have always loved my Grandmother; her soft smile, her gentle touch. This was a woman who loved everything and everyone. Surprisingly, to this day, my love for her remains unreciprocated, for I only knew her early in life. Her existence, etched in my mind, persists with me. She was a beautiful woman. Ironically, her most beautiful moment was one over which she had no control. That moment was the result of her death: her funeral.

It was a bitterly cold winter's day. The sun above could not be found, probably cowering behind ominous blankets of gray. The wind was still, the rotation of the earth halted, and all creatures took breath in anticipation. The world was still.

Looking toward the boat, I notice my family funnel aboard. Fighting the crowd, my dad pushes to the end of the boat. "It won't be long now" he yells, but not to me, in reassurance to himself. Looking down I began to nod, "Yes, yes," then I reached out, grasped a reed tightly, and thrust it deep within my pocket. I treated it as if it were a wild animal, and if loose, it would escape and never be seen again. I stood up. Proceeding up the ramp to the boat, I was the last one to enter.

I searched for comfort and support: my parents. I found my mom first, standing towards the back of the boat. She stood, watching dry land run away from her. She stared, as if, were she to blink, home would disappear forever; lost in the vastness that is the ocean. I stood beside her, and grasped her hand tightly. She squeezed in response. Here eyes red from crying, she cannot hide. Sunken, a great weight exudes from her. She moves slowly and painfully; meticulously, as though made of glass. Small tremors assault her hands; stop only when grasped by an other. My mother

39

is beautiful. I leave her, hesitantly, and make my way to the bow of the boat.

Upon arrival I grasp the railing. The boat accelerates, thus causing the "nose" to hop up and down over intersecting wakes in the ocean. It was a game. The boat, the bull, the rail was my reigns; grasping tightly I didn't dare let go, for it would almost certainly mean annihilation. I was a child, innocent, and carefree. An escapist caught in a boyhood fantasy. Bucking, swaying . . . the crowd cheered me on. This hull was a beast, but I could weather the storm. Nothing was going to knock me off.

Seconds later my father grabbed my shoulder, and pulled. "We're almost there" his voice trailed off. I let go of the reigns. Back to reality. We trudged, side by side, to a room inside. I left my childhood at the bow of the boat.

Stepping inside I noticed that I was last to enter. There were rows of folding chairs facing an old weathered man standing next to an urn containing my late grandmother's ashes. My seat was in the back, behind the tallest of our family. I decided not to worry. I figured there wasn't anything to see. Then I remembered. I felt within my pocket and triumphantly found my prize. It still remained in my possession, it hadn't escaped. The proceedings continued. The old man spoke, and some gave speeches. Everyone sobbed. Then at the direction of the old man, everyone vacated. We gathered as a family at the side of the boat, one love, one spirit. One person.

The captain, a tall lanky man, held my grandmother in a box. Slowly he walked through the crowd. Like holding hot water, the man didn't falter, he was calm and composed. The sobbing escalated as he approached the side of the boat. This was the final good bye. Louder. Everyone held one another, holding them tight. The captain placed the container in an intricately woven Venetian basket. Next he turned to us. He spoke, but no one listened. Smothered by the collective sobs, everyone stared in anticipation.

40

His voice broke through the commotion "And to you, we bid you farewell."

The basket lowered. A slight breeze sent the basket a-sway. Like the watch of a hypnotist, the basket lulled us into eerie calm. All was quiet. Finally, after what seemed like years, of intense observation, the basket touched down. Rapid concentric dark blue circles rippled from beneath the oceanic coffin. As the basket sank, wave upon wave rushed within. The sudden rush sent a small stream of water and vibrant rose petals careening towards the sky. The pedals danced and spun in the light breeze. Then, sinking further, the remaining vivid petals seeped out to open ocean. The yellows, whites, and reds scattered consistently, each with its own agenda. The scene was too much, our party dissolved into tears. Then I remembered. Reaching down, I pulled the flower from the depths of my pocket. The long, slender green stem, bent from my pocket, led to a simple yellow dandelion; simple in composition, powerful by intention. I was a child, innocent, carefree, and loving. I tossed the flower into the ocean. "I love you grandma" was all I was able to choke out. The scene was too much, the heavens exploded in tears; bullets from above pierced the ocean.

Our family funneled back inside. I looked around; everyone looked dazed and confused; tired and excited. The events that had unfolded had caught everyone off guard, catching people at their weakest moments. We looked vulnerable, but we had each other. We were a true family. We were beautiful.

However, to understand what beauty truly is, one must understand what it isn't. Beauty isn't vanity or prosperity or popularity or success. Beauty cannot be bought or manufactured in any sense of the word. Yet, beauty can be found everywhere. Beauty entitles vulnerability, and trust. *Beauty is the raw representation of life.*

Ryan Marr
Author/ Student
Los Alamitos High School
IdealSelf@aol.com

41

For your free gift, go to: **www.wakeupand.com**

42

Shake It Up
David Larner

It was 4:31a.m. on January 17, 1994 and my family was fast asleep in their beds when all hell broke loose. The ground moved, the walls started to shake and the noise was deafening. We were in the middle of a major earthquake and, as we would find out later, our house in Northridge, California, was at ground zero. Suddenly, we had no hot water, no electricity, and you could put your hand through the newly-formed opening between the top of the living room wall and the roofline.

For the next several months we walked through the house in fear of aftershocks. Once things began to settle down, we packed up everything we had and placed our furniture in storage. We then moved to a small drafty apartment and began what we thought would be a few months of repairs. But it turned into a ten-month ordeal that required us to rebuild our house from the studs up.

I remember driving to Home Depot at 2:00 a.m. in a vicious rainstorm to buy plastic tarps so I could cover the studs of my exposed house. "My life is out of control," I thought. "It just can't get any worse."

But it did get worse. I lost my job of fifteen years. We struggled on my wife's income and relied on our savings to help us get by. Then my wife's employer went into bankruptcy. Her stock became worthless and we were on the ropes.

I had to do something fast. Unemployed and desperate, I moved into action. Fortunately, I've always had an entrepreneurial spirit. During my formative years I had created several financially successful businesses. Even when I was in elementary school I purchased candy bars by the box and resold them on the playground to the other kids.

I began my own technology-marketing firm. The Internet was really beginning to take off at that time, and life began to turn

43

around. I was back in the entrepreneurial life that I loved. For the next several years I worked on growing my business.

Today, the inherent flexibility of self-employment allows me to attend my son's school events and sports activities. I've even coached several of his league teams. No longer governed by fixed vacation schedules and limited days off, we travel to Europe, Alaska, Canada and other memorable locations. I am now a published author, speaker and consultant and the seemingly difficult set of circumstances that brought me to this point have allowed me to *Live the Life I Love!*

David Larner
Internet Marketing Expert
dlarner@tmcla.com
www.tmcla.com
For a Free Website Review Call (818) 986-7200

44

Hard Work And Learning Are My Friends
Tom Antion

These words of wisdom from my Father have served me well for many years. I rented an apartment as a college student. My Father told me to learn everything that I could, so I began following my landlord around when he came to check on the apartments. I would help him with maintenance and repairs for free just to learn all about the apartment business. When he decided to retire, he told me that I was the hardest working young man he knew and that he would carry the financing if I wanted to take over the business. So, by the time that I finished college, I owned five apartment buildings and a hotel and knew how to run a property investment business.

This lesson and venture in my early days has served me well, especially when mixed with a desire to live the life you love. I've made it a point in my life to work only on things I enjoy. I'll scrape and crawl to find a way to earn money by doing things that excite me, challenge me, and satisfy my desire to help someone besides myself.

When you work only on things you love to do, it is easy to achieve excellence because your work doesn't feel like work. It's enjoyable to put in the extra time necessary to really excel at what you are doing. This excellence shows through and makes people want to use your services.

As Mark Twain said, "Work consists of whatever a body is obliged to do; Play consists of whatever a body is not obliged to do." If you just realize what it is that you really love, you will find that the world will pay you to play.

Everything I've accomplished in my life, from owning an outrageous practical joke company to being known, now, as the top

45

LIVE THE LIFE YOU LOVE

Internet marketing expert in my industry, has come from "playing" hard and continually learning about the things I love.

Tom Antion
tom@antion.com
www.antion.com
www.public-speaking.org

46

In Sickness and In Health
Dr. Jackie Black

I am a proud mother, successful professional, good friend and avid traveler. Yet my heart was closed to a deeply meaningful and loving relationship with a man. But who knew? I was at the home of a friend and…he arrived.

He is as compelling to me today, as he was the moment I met him. He still gets butterflies when I walk into a room. His name is Mark. He changed my life forever. Living the life I love with the love of my life is remarkably amazing, rewarding and challenging.

We are partners and companions, peers, teammates, cohorts, lovers and best friends. We waited our entire lives to find each other. We melt at each other's touch, respect one another's points of view, and freely express our joy and appreciation for each other. Feedback and opinions are usually welcome and we are regularly tickled and delighted by each other. And oh yes, we occasionally disagree vigorously.

A few weeks before our wedding we found out his cancer came back. The day after our wedding he started chemotherapy that knocked out the cancer and almost took him with it. Cancer free! But he was so sick for so long we hardly had a chance to enjoy it. Then the cancer came back. A "bigger" chemotherapy this time, but without the terrible side affects. Again, cancer free …until it came back. Today, a highly experimental drug is working its magic!

Through it all, we are graced by the presence of each other and the joyfulness we feel just being in the same room or riding around in our golf cart. Mostly, we don't waste time worrying about a future we cannot control. We honor the promise of today and savor being loved by and loving each other.

We are deeply grateful that we found each other. We rejoice in the wisdom that allowed us to abandon our fears from the past,

47

put aside our concerns about the future and act with courage to live in the present and welcome love into our hearts. For however long he is on this planet, I am forever enriched by being loved by him, loving him and sharing my life with him.

Jackie Black, Ph.D.
California
www.DrJackieBlack.com
DrJackie@DrJackieBlack.com
888.792.6224

48

The Clown That Outwitted Confucius
Mike Fry

In late fall of 1987 I had a "crazy idea" that forever changed my life. While eating in my favorite small, Chinese restaurant, I wondered "Why doesn't anyone make fortune cookies in fun colors and flavors that actually taste good?"

I was tired of my fortune cookies tasting bland, in one flavor and sometimes almost cardboard-like in taste. So, I decided to pioneer the idea and take on the challenge myself. Cold logic should have warned me about how hard my unusual idea would be to pull off.

In fact, that "out of the box" idea has become my life's work for the last 15 years! And it's taken me on a magical journey into the mysterious fortune cookie making world.

I left my job as a professional Ringling Bros. and Barnum & Bailey circus clown. Yes! I was a clown with the "Greatest Show on Earth." And then, I quit my own children's TV show that had been airing in 209 cities on FOX eight years in a row.

But, I was absolutely determined that my flavoring idea was a good one. So, I turned in my notice and left my job in October of 1990 to the shock and laughter of my family, the TV station and my friends. Who would want to buy "flavored" fortune cookies made by a former clown, everybody jokingly kept asking me.

Little did I know that I was trying to break into one of the most unusual and secretive food industries you could imagine. In fact, I was literally the first non-Chinese person to ever begin actually making and manufacturing fortune cookies in gourmet flavors and colors.

I called 8 different Chinese fortune cookie companies back in 1987, and tried unsuccessfully to find any one of them that thought my idea of flavors and colors was a good idea. Finally, the ninth manufacturer was willing to listen to me. For the next 2 years we painstakingly experimented and created mountains of bad looking and bad tasting fortune cookies until one day, we "cracked the code."

Today I manufacture 17 flavors and colors you can customize with your own personal messages inside for special events, tradeshows or even weddings.

My advice is to take that fun and crazy dream you have and risk people laughing at you. Remember...

"He who not take risk may not get reward."

Mike Fry
317-299-8900
www.fancyfortunecookies.com

50

All Win
Judge William Huss

Conflict is a constant part of our lives. When we want something and an obstacle is put in our way, we have conflict. How we resolve a conflict reveals much about who we are. From infancy, we are taught ways to resolve conflict enabling us to carry on cultural values in our lives. For example, there was a time when our American culture required us to go to arbitration or trial to solve our problems. Now mediation is being used more and more instead. Obviously, there are still cases that can only be resolved by a court or an arbitration and an inevitable part of this process is that someone has to lose. These situations generally result in:

A negative embrace
   A requirement of blame
      A loss difficult to heal and never forgotten
         A destruction of personal and business relationships

Today, many people are negotiating or mediating their disputes before they even file a lawsuit, preventing unnecessary stress on their finances and their psyches. They promote:

The healing of relationships
   The avoidance of letting others make important decisions
      The sharing of important decision making
         The feeling of satisfaction from personal accomplishment

After leaving the bench where I was responsible for determining who was right and who was wrong, I began devoting my time to mediation, the search for ways for all to win in any dispute. I am so grateful that I did. Thanks to mediation, countless relationships and money has been spared and countless individuals are able to pursue their goals and dreams without the burden of a lawsuit hanging over their heads. My decision to mediate made my life better, in large measure, because I know that it has improved others' lives as well.

Judge William Huss
Co-author of:
Working with Your Homeowners Association; A Guide for Living
Author of the forthcoming book:
Shake On It; Mediating your Way To Success

My Dad, My Hero
Dr. Shailendra Kumar

It was early spring. Basking in the fresh morning air under a Neem tree, there he was doing his Yoga exercises. Sirsasana was his particular favorite, and he did it with utmost ease as he modeled it for me. As an eminent scholar and a university professor, my Pitaji wrote many books on philosophy, poetry and culture, guided students doing graduate research in literature, presided over major conferences and gave talks on the radio. As he walked down the streets, people greeted him with respect.

And yet, at one time this was simply a dream for a boy who lost his father at the age of two; who was growing up in a small village with no electricity or running water. Nevertheless, studying under a kerosene lamp, he saw a different world in his mind's eyes. While his peers settled for mediocrity, this warrior found a way to escape to Mathura, a nearby city, to go to school and then to college.

The road was challenging with studies, a job and, later on, a family to care for. The burden was intense and, one day, he fainted from overwork. But the fire within and the faith in divine power only got stronger. Pitaji went on to earn double Masters (Hindi and Sanskrit), a Ph. D. and then, the most coveted degree, Doctor of Literature. He was simply unstoppable.

During my childhood, we lived in a modest home, but there was plenty of love. One incident is particularly memorable when he took me to watch a Cricket "Test Match" in Delhi. We sat together for five days watching the game. It was a priceless gift – a unique gift of time with him. Over and over he told me that my riches were between my two ears and in my heart, and that no one could ever take those away from me.

On religious occasions he would have the family together, invite neighbors, and did poojas – prayers to gods and goddesses. This devotee never forgot the source of his power – the Almighty God, and honored Him. When I was leaving for the U.S., he told me very lovingly, "With God, you can accomplish anything!"

"In my own quest for learning, I have been attracted to the teachings of many masters. And yet, as I look back I realize that some of the most important lessons I have ever learned came from my Dad — lessons in faith, persistence, and unconditional love.

Pitaji, you are my hero, always have been, always will! How fortunate I am to have a father like you.

Dr. Shailendra Kumar
www.DrShailendraKumar.com

54

Footnotes:
   Neem is an herb used in Ayurvedic medicine for many ailments.
   Sirsasana is a unique Yoga posture in which one stands on his head upside down with hands providing lateral support

Desire, Dream, Decision
Sam Pelicon

You must have a clear dream. And when you dream,
look at where you want to be—not where you are.
Don't work harder; dream bigger.
If I knew that all of my dreams would come true,
I would just dream bigger.

I remember working hard when I started in a network marketing business. I didn't sleep (except for Saturdays) for eight months. I worked all night with pizzas and newspapers and worked my network business all day. For transportation, I got a car from the scrap yard. But, after eight months, I could get on an airplane and leave Canada.

I had worked for IBM and I was a computer specialist. I was looking for a good job, but without success. However, when I thought about it, I didn't really want a job no matter how well they paid; I wanted to be my own boss.

When you're the boss, even if you lose all of your money, you can take the knowledge you have gained and build it all back. Well, I had it all planned in my mind. This is the only country where you can make it from rags to riches.

You must have a desire, a dream and make a decision. And you must never give up on your dreams. Never, never, never give up on your dreams.

That all-consuming desire is something I discuss often. At I meeting in Hawaii, a lady asked me, "What is this 'burning desire' you talk about? Can you show me an example?" So, we went out into the ocean. I asked her how long she could hold her breath. "About two minutes," she said. So, with her cooperation, I held her head under the water for one — two — almost 3 minutes! She came up gasping and said, "What are you trying to do? Drown me?"

"No," I answered. "I wanted you to experience the kind of desire that you must have if you will succeed. When you were under the water during that last minute, your only desire was to get air. You had a burning desire for air. Now you know how it feels."

Most people never know true, burning desire. Do you?

Desire, dreams and firm commitment.

Sam Pelicon
spelicon@hotmail.com
Executive Vice President, MSTGS

56

To Be Human
Reg Athwal

It can take years for people to realize their purposes on this planet. When the breakthrough happens, it is because the right questions are asked. What are my God-given talents? What do I love to do? What can I create? Who am I and what can I become? Once these questions are answered, boom! Their lives change in a heartbeat. So why did it have to take so long?

When I was 19 years-old, I addressed an audience of 3,000 sales representatives. My raw, non-rehearsed style impressed many, and the response was phenomenal. People were convinced that I was a seasoned public speaker. I remember moving around the stage with the words flowing out with passion and energy. The message filled the room, bouncing from person to person, gathering momentum, and picking up the audience's emotions and excitement along the way. It felt amazing, but from where had this intensity emerged? I couldn't fathom how that magical feeling of enlightenment turned into 10 years of my life. My ability to speak presented itself in small doses, disguised in different outfits, but I kept ignoring the signs.

Sound familiar?

The feeling is amazing when the gates are opened. In a moment of enlightened illumination, I found my purpose for being on this planet. It happened to me in the midst of a business break-up. My life was filled with chaos and tremendous dissatisfaction. During this time, I made a decision to become a professional speaker who would educate, inspire and empower people to turn their undiscovered talents and potential into reality. My life's purpose was suddenly born and was to be expressed through my natural speaking abilities.

Fortunately, I discovered my purpose near my thirtieth birthday. Looking around, I see people who are still ignoring the signs, the messages from the universal spirit, the constant tapping in the mind that is saying "Hey you! Yes, you. Are you living the life you really love? Are you expressing your talents or are you living your life for someone else? Living the life of fear?" The tapping persists and once it gets through, the new message is "Yes! Go on, jump! You can do it, don't fear anymore! I'll support you. Live your dreams! Become the artist, the instructor, the speaker, the entertainer, the joker, the inventor, the musician, the writer, the singer, the celebrity, the traveler, the lover, the parent, the designer, or the healer. Stop pretending to be someone else and be who you really are!"

We enter this world with nothing and leave with nothing. The journey in between is meant to be wonderful, full of creation, joy, growth, love, contribution, discovery, energy, possibility, adventure, purpose, and life. Our lives must consist of this for us to be content. Remove controlling egos, negative beliefs, physical features and possessions. What do we really have left? We have each other as mankind, all the wonderful aspects that make up nature, our senses, our thoughts, our energies, our silence, and our collective consciousness.

What is it to be human? It is to rediscover these basic principles, to appreciate them, and to live the life we love.

"To be human is to fully exist like the sun.
Energy is flowing in motions of learning and ready for fun.
Make up your mind to be a part of this journey.
A path of rediscovery and creation is yearning."

Reg Athwal
CEO, RAW LTD, Surrey, England
Author, Speaker, Trainer, Entrepreneur
Co-author *The Inspirational Poet*
www.regathwal.com

Buckle Up, Somebody Loves You
In Memory of Jeffrey "Wolf" Winton
Pam Fahey

Losing a 16-year-old son in a tragic car accident could be a reason to stop living. Please, buckle up and save a life.

Jeff was the third child out of four and was always sweet, caring and very thoughtful. He went out of his way to make sure all around him had what they needed, even if it meant sacrificing himself.

We believe that Jeff's friendships were very important in his life. With great friends, everything else came easier making Jeff a contented young man who lived life to the fullest. His message could not be more clearly stated than it was in this poem written shortly before his death:

> *If you've lost money,*
> > *you've lost nothing.*
> *If you've lost honor,*
> > *you've lost a lot.*
> *If you've lost courage,*
> > *you've lost the world.*
> *If you've lost friendship,*
> > *you've lost everything.*
>
> *Jeff Winton (1980-1997)*

Jeff's untimely death "woke" our family making us realize the importance of each day and each relationship. His death helped us to keep sight of our purposes instead of getting caught up in the "rat race."

Jeff touched the hearts of everyone he met during his life. He continues to touch hearts in his death through his story, *The Boy*

59

They Called Wolf, available at www.truestoriesonline.com. Take a look, I am certain that Jeff's story will give your life new meaning and focus.

Remember, a long life is never guaranteed, but a full life is within your reach.

Pamela Fahey
Wife, mother, grandmother, entrepreneur
www.truestoriesonline.com
pam.@truestoriesonline.com

60

Be Smart…Incorporate Your Business and Have Financial Freedom
Gil Kim

No matter what your present circumstances, the first step to your financial freedom is the commitment to having it. What if I met you 100 years ago and told you that someday almost every single home will have something called a computer? You would probably think I was crazy. Returning to the present, what if I told you that every intelligent person will incorporate his or her business? Does that seem crazy? Not if you understand what it means to be incorporated. It is a process that the wealthy already know and what everyone else should learn. (For more information on incorporation, check www.mstgs.com).

Aside from incorporating your own business, it is important to keep these other things in mind when striving to become wealthy:

61

* *Be self-employed*
* *Have a product that benefits people*
* *Work with good people*
* *Share your wealth with the people that help you*
* *Do not be afraid to make decisions*

* *Be focused until the end of the project and understand that you will have distractions along the way*
* *Understand the power of leverage*
* *Focus on the solution, not the problem*
* *Remove "can't" from your vocabulary*
* *Hire smart people*
* *Understand that your words manifest your reality*
* *Make other people's dreams come true*

For your free gift, go to: **www.wakeupand.com**

LIVE THE LIFE YOU LOVE

* *Think BIG*
* *Build a strong foundation*
* *Spend time in prayer*

And finally, a piece of advice that comes from a very smart young man, my eleven year-old son, George Kim:

"Focus on your dreams coming true, not those of someone else."

Gil Kim
President and CEO, MSTG Solution
www.mstgs.com

62

The Power of a Core Desire
Dr. Jason Gospodarek

It all started in early high school.

I was born and raised in a small northeastern Wisconsin town of fewer than 1500 people and at age 13 I began working on a large dairy farm. As I matured, my employers gave me more important responsibilities, including tasks that challenged my body and mind. Just as my body was growing during my years at the farm, so were my morals and values. My experience taught me not only respect for others, but for the environment and other life around me as well.

One muggy summer morning it hit me. I was sweeping along the feeding area when one of my co-workers pulled along side of me in his tractor.

"How's it going today?" he asked.

"Not too bad," I replied, "Just another day."

"I hear that," he yawned, "I can't wait to get outta here today. If they paid me more, I could at least go home and have something to show for it all. I guess that's just another notch in the 20 year belt at the farm..."

As he drove away that morning, I knew my life had changed. I thought to myself, "How could I stand to stay here any longer? There are people here doing the same work as I, making only a few more dollars an hour, and all they do is complain."

I took the easiest possible course load during my senior year in high school. Even though I was not very interested in continuing my education, I decided to try a year at the local community college just to see how things would "turn out". Well it "turned out" that I made the Dean's List and decided to push myself even harder.

I attended a college of about 8,000 students and earned my bachelors degree in biology with a minor in chemistry. I then chose to pursue a doctorate at the Indiana University School of Optometry where I graduated with honors.

63

Now, I have returned to Wisconsin and enjoy practicing optometry in a beautiful clinic on a Native American reservation. As things settle in my life, I continue to re-solidify the relationships with family and friends that weakened with the distance and stresses of my education.

With the demands of eight years of college behind me, I feed off the spark that was ignited within me on that hot summer morning years ago on the farm. Thanks to that morning, I have started several small businesses and continue to explore and enjoy life to its absolute fullest each day. I also help others, via the Internet, find personal and professional fulfillment in their own lives.

As I look back on my life, I believe that my humble beginnings have shaped the life I live today. The key to fulfillment is to realize your core desires, as these desires are the fuel for the roots of your existence in day-to-day life. Discover these desires, unleash them, and you too can discover the extraordinary forces that lie within you.

Dr. Jason Gospodarek
Optometrist, Success Coach, and Author
Jason@InnovativeCoaching.com
www.InnovativeCoaching.com
www.JasonGospodarek.com
www.TheAnxietyAnswer.com

64

Live Your Dreams
Clint Sloan

*"And then you reach out into the beautiful deep blue
as the dolphin glides by and touches your hands."*

5:30 a.m. and you're violently awakened by an annoying sound that you purposely create for yourself each night before you go to sleep. Any remembrance of a dream is quickly wiped away by the routine that you have acquired during the past several years.

Your suit is not quite pressed and your hair is making you crazy after seeing it in the rearview mirror. You glance to see how angry is the driver that you cut off because you're late for work.

You don't think much as you enter your workplace; you react. As the day comes to an end you think, "If only he would have said, 'The Moon,' the contestant would have won the jackpot, the ultimate dream, on Who Wants to be a Millionaire." Of course, you're thinking all this while your boss is yelling and degrading you again because you didn't quite meet your quota.

Night falls, but you can't quite rest due to the heartburn from a fast food meal and your distress because your Three Hundred Dollar tax refund hasn't come in the mail yet.

5:30 a.m. and you are wakened by a soft, beautiful sound. It's a tropical bird, one that you heard before. But this morning it sounds just a little different because the surf has calmed under the peaceful trades.

The sun slowly rises, creating an incredible array of colors. As you bite into your fresh fruit, you get to see the first sparkle on the ocean as the sun kisses the waves. You slip on your suit and you journey out to one of your favorite places to see if today you will be blessed with the opportunity to swim with your wonderful friends.

The tropical breeze feels great through your hair and, as you dive into the water, the dolphins send you a warm "hello."

65

Late that afternoon you go to your studio and you create a painting from all the inspiration of the day. As night falls, the full moon rises and casts a magical light through the windows of your bedroom. You rest your head on the big, fluffy pillow and slip into an incredible dream; you reach out into the beautiful deep blue as the dolphin glides by and touches your hands.

As a child I loved to draw and, as I grew older, I continued to follow that passion. Today my paintings sell around the world and I have created a freedom that I cherish each and every day.

Many said, "Being an artist is unrealistic." "Keep it as a hobby, but get a real job." "You're a DREAMER!"

I'm proud to say that I am a dreamer, and if you haven't done it yet, I wish for you to reach out and touch the dolphins.

*Why let others color your world
when you have your own crayons?*

Clint Sloan
www.clintsloan.com

66

You are Your Best Investment
Lynn Pierce

Always be an active learner. The more you invest in yourself, the more confidently you will make decisions. Some of the most important decisions you will make in your life will have to be made in an instant.

I never expected to be using the information I learned to deal with cancer.

I have spent many years learning what makes people do what they do and what makes them change. Whether reading a book, listening to tapes or attending seminars, I am constantly learning how to be the best me I can be. I've studied sales and marketing, personal development, the mind/body connection and also developed an interest in health and nutrition.

In May of 1999, while living in a small town in Mexico, my world was rocked by a diagnosis of breast cancer. The knowledge I had in my own personal library, and the beliefs I developed from what I had learned, made it possible for me to deal with the situation and triumph over it.

I used that situation as a catalyst to change my life completely. I've always believed you write the script for your own life. If you don't, you'll be living someone else's script.

You must create a vision of what you want your life to look like. Break down your vision into an action plan with steps you will take to make it a reality. Now get to work on it.

The script I continue to write for myself allows me to live in warm sunny resort areas, moving where I want and when I want. I do the work that I love. It's my passion. How did I create this life and why is it so easy for me to manifest it?

I used the steps I just gave you. With just three simple steps you can be living the life you love. Have a dream. Create a vision and make it happen. Then live it. There's my motto: *"Dream It,*

67

Create It, Live It!"

Investing in yourself gives you knowledge. Knowledge gives you power to make intelligent choices. Just remember, if you don't invest in you, who will?

Lynn Pierce
The Sales Therapist
Author: *Getting to YES Without Selling*
www.changeonething.com
480-242-5929

68

The Three Magic O's
Michael Levine

OPTIMISM • OBSESSION • OBLIGATION

What is the secret of a winner? It's simple: The Three Magic O's. If you work tirelessly on these Three Magic O's, you will not only succeed; you will triumph and prosper in a way you cannot even imagine. Guaranteed.

The secret to the Three Magic O's is simple. Not easy... *simple*.

Excellence in one or two O's is not enough. Success demands all three. They must be practiced together.

They must be practiced consistently. Every day. Weekends too.

They must be practiced especially when you feel overwhelmed or stressed. That is when they have the most significance.

They must be monitored. Check yourself on the Magic O's daily, weekly, monthly. What we measure gets done.

Optimism

Optimistic: Positive, encouraging, upbeat, enthusiastic, energetic, grateful, non-complaining.

Having a positive, enthusiastic attitude is a key component of the Three Magic O's. Push yourself to be the most positive, optimistic, enthusiastic person you know.

Optimism does not mean unrealistic or saccharin sweet or goodie-goodie. It means to believe deeply in the possibility that with enough hard work, tomorrow can be better than today. General Colin Powell said it best in only six words: "Perpetual optimism is a force multiplier."

Obsession

Obsession: Burning maniacal commitment, total focus, determination, unrelenting resourcefulness. Whatever it takes, with no excuses, treating every task as though your life depended on it.

Think of the word "obsession"— it conveys a strong image. It can be described as a burning, maniacal passion to accomplish something. Imagine the level of intensity, determination, and creativity you would bring to a problem if your life or the life of a loved one depended on it.

Obsession demands of you to do whatever it takes. That is why they call it obsession. Get it?

Obligation

Obligation: Tenacity, determination, discipline, honor, keeping promises.

Winners are promise-keepers. They say what they mean and mean what they say. Because their word is good, people quickly learn they can be trusted. They are not flaky. Flake is another word for loser. Flakes ask for vacation time during job interviews.

On the other hand, promise-keepers see their tasks as commitments, not merely things to be done only if they are easy. They assign a sense of honor and responsibility to all they do.

The key to obligation is self-discipline. Approach all your obstacles with the best of your ability, despite your feelings or the inconvenience.

Get it straight: Success is inconvenient, tiring, and time-consuming, among many other things. Get used to it! Losers quit when they are tired; winners quit when they have won. Winners see their work as obligation; not as a burden, but as responsibility to themselves and others. Nevertheless, winners are not ruled entirely by their feelings. Acting responsibly prior to feeling responsible builds character.

The sooner you start the process of constantly applying and measuring the Three Magic O's, the sooner your life will change for the better – not easier, but better. Good luck. Now it is up to you.

Michael Levine
Levine Communications Office
michael@levinepr.com
www.levinepr.com

For your free gift, go to: **www.wakeupand.com**

How Do You Know?
Todd Canedy

How do you know? —There's a saying...

> *"It's not what you don't know that's dangerous,
> it's what you think you know, and don't?"*

I like this statement because it has two strong messages. First, we are not capable of knowing everything and therefore should not make an attempt to try to know everything. It also reminds us of a cardinal virtues of mankind: prudence. Prudence is the mother of clarity and certainty. It is pivotal in reaching desired results. Prudence forces you to ask, "How do I know?"

Let's pretend that you are facing a monumental decision. The outcome of this decision will have a significant impact on your life. Make the right decision and life will greatly improve. Make the wrong decision and life will be terribly disappointing at best. There seems to be no middle ground.

Thankfully, there are many outcomes we can expect if we are prudent and examine the situation carefully. However, just because these outcomes are expected does not necessarily guarantee that they will be the ones you desire. Before making any decision it is important to ask yourself these preliminary questions:

➤ What am I going to change?
➤ What am I changing it to?
➤ How am I going to cause the change to happen?

Life changing actions are best executed when you determine what exactly it is you want. For example, it is tempting for people to dwell on why they are unhappy because determining what makes us miserable is much easier than figuring out how to improve our lives. This is fruitless, and puts you in a dark backward thinking realm.

- ➤ Start by asking yourself what happiness means to you.
- ➤ Determine what has to change to get there.
- ➤ Make a plan to cause the change.

There is an old adage that says "Fortune favors the bold… and the prudent." Try attacking your goals prudently and you are guaranteed to find what it is you are seeking.

Todd Canedy
email: canedyt@sbcglobal.net
714-695-0221

72

You Never Know and the Rest Is History!
Lou and Carla Ferrigno

I was taking a break from being a therapist, and was managing a TGI Fridays restaurant when I was called to the front door one night. A very large 300 pound man was standing there taking up the entire doorway. He was really taken back because I was a woman and the manager. He asked if they could be seated even though some of the guys were under age. Because we had an open bar, I told him that was not possible. He asked several times, but I would not allow them to be seated. My staff came running to me when he left, because they knew who Lou was and they said, "how could you do that." They could not believe that I had thrown out "The Incredible Hulk". I had never seen his show.

The following Friday evening, he returned with his stunt double. Now I didn't remember who he was from the time before but as I passed by his table, he asked if I would sit down and talk with him. Since I was the only woman manager with TGIF at the time, I made it a policy to never sit down and visit with the restaurant patrons. As I came by the table again, he asked if I would sit down with them and again I said no. However, he kept asking and his eyes were just so sweet, I finally sat down for a few minutes. I never dated men that were big, Italians or Scorpio.

He asked if he could take me to breakfast and I said no. He told me he had a party with Dolly Parton to attend and wanted me to go with him. I told him no. He asked for my phone number and I told him no. Again after he persisted, I took his number and I told him I might call him. You guessed it! I did call him and as they say, *the rest is history.*

The next day, after the party, I told my mother that I had met the man that I was going to marry. We were never apart from that time on. Now 24 years and three wonderful children later, I love

73

the entertainment and training business, however, my greatest joy is my life with Lou and our family.

Carla Ferrigno
Author: *Women Only: Carla Ferrigno's Total Shape-Up Program*
Over 20 years as certified fitness trainer
Movies: *Black Roses* and *The Seven Magnificent Gladiators*

Lou Ferrigno
Guiness Book of world records as the youngest Mr. Universe
and the only 2 time consectitive winner.
Author: *Lou Ferrigno's Guide to Personal Power, Bodybuilding and Fitness*
Television appearances include a recurring role on *The King of Queens*
Over 20 feature films including: *Pumping Iron,
The Seven Magnificent Gladiators, Hercules* and *The Adventures of Hercules*

74

Living the Life I Love
Orrin C. Hudson

I consider myself very fortunate to be able to live a life I love. My brother taught me to play chess several years ago, as a young man, but I didn't develop a love for the game until 1996. I entered my first tournament in 1997 and lost. Despite my disappointment, I gained a valuable lesson from an opponent. He told me to study the games of the best players. After losing again in 1998, I asked the State Champion what I could do to improve my game. He was generous with his time and shared some valuable insights.

I learned that "success leaves clues." Library cards are free and the Birmingham library had eight million dollars worth of information available to me. I began my crusade to turn children and adults into readers with the message that "readers become leaders." I volunteered to help people to improve their reading skills while I worked on my chess skills with a 10-time winner of the Birmingham Chess Tournament.

I entered the Birmingham Chess Tournament again in 1999. The morning the tournament began, I told the tournament director that he could go ahead and give me my trophy because I planned to win. He laughed and told me that while I could learn from my experience, he didn't think I'd have a chance since I was the lowest seeded player in the event. When I took first place, everyone was shocked. Then, the reaction was that it was sheer luck.

When I took first place again the following year, I knew I could teach the most important lesson in life while I taught chess. You never know what you can do, until you try. Within months, plans to turn my dream into the *Be Someone* organization were realized.

Chess is a metaphor for life. For your life to get better, you have to get better. You are responsible for your own decisions and must handle the consequences. You must see the game clearly, plan your moves wisely, and be prepared for the unexpected. Every day I have

75

the opportunity to help others build their self-confidence, improve their skills, and enjoy life.

After all, each person I meet can "be someone."

Orrin C. Hudson
President
Be Someone, Inc.
7148 Stonebrook Lane
Lithonia, GA 30058
770-484-1887
orrin@besomeone.org
www.besomeone.org

76

Waking Up
Pamela Samantha Michaels

Perhaps the most important question is, "*Do you have the courage — the guts — to live fully, present in a life you don't want?*"

Now, don't get me wrong.. When we begin to live our dreams, there is a magic that occurs which is utterly breathtaking. To do so at all is to do so with power, intentionality and joy. There is no excuse, as we emerge now into the era of enlightenment in the fast lane, not to live at our fullest potential and most sizzling aliveness; to hold on to any portion of ourselves that does not speak of our clearest truth.

Life happens. Sometimes, despite our best efforts to actualize the *Life We Want,* we create something we didn't bargain for. And at these times we are asked to let go; to rest in a deeper consecration and trust; to know that this, too, is Divine.

Our souls often choose challenges for us that may be unacceptable to your ego. Yet, these challenges invariably present the greatest opportunities for growth and true surrender. In my own life, at the height of actualizing *What I Wanted,* I was given the unspeakable gift of a disabled child. None of my spiritual training or psychological education could possibly have prepared me for such a challenge, and I raged against God, against my Soul; this was not my will. But perhaps, at a deeper level, it was. As I have been asked daily to go through fires, fires of brutality and exquisite beauty, fires which demanded surrender, much of my former self and my illusions have been burned away. Now, I live in gratitude, and understand that nothing I consciously chose could have possibly taught me more about Love, or granted me such Grace.

Paradoxically, it is only in yielding to a higher wisdom that we begin to truly live a life of spontaneity and fluidity, to truly wake up and live the life we want. When we are in our centers, embracing with all our hearts whatever Is, there is less resistance, fear or need to

77

control, and we move out of a simple, pure state that naturally
expresses our highest dreams and creates in perfect concert with the
world. As we soften to the moment, without attachment or
expectation, our presence is radiant with exuberance and right
action, genuineness and integrity.

And what more could we want?

Pamela Samantha Michaels
Wellness Coach
e-mail quark220@adelphia.net
phone 805-427-2297

78

LIVE THE LIFE YOU LOVE

Stop Looking and Live It
Wing Lam

Fourteen years ago, I set a goal to start a restaurant that extended from my home. I imagined having friends over for a big party and serving delicious food. My vision was to create a playful environment so that, when the patrons left, they would tell their friends about it and visit again. When I began devising this plan, people told me I was crazy and that it would never work.

They were wrong. Fourteen years ago, I started Wahoo's Fish Taco and now own 28 locations with nearly 500 employees.

My advice to anyone who is hesitant to pursue a dream would be to walk through your fears. Nobody knows you are scared and when you become successful, people will assume that you are an expert. Those who succeed rarely do it on knowledge alone. It takes courage and determination to go past the fear and put that knowledge to work. Success and opportunity are not only for some people, it is available to anyone. Stop looking and start living. *Take action now!*

I can also contribute my success to mentors who have guided me through my business endeavor. I hold my father, who taught me the value of hard work, and my great friend and life coach, John Carpenter, responsible for helping me achieve my goals. I would advise anyone who wants to succeed to make sure they have a mentor to help them along the way.

Here are a just a few pointers that I believe will help you live the life you love:

> 🐟 Just do it
> 🐟 Your beauty is within
> 🐟 Spend time in nature
> 🐟 Go surfing
> 🐟 Give back to the community

79

For your free gift, go to: **www.wakeupand.com**

WAKE UP!!!
LIVE THE LIFE YOU LOVE

- Do not procrastinate
- Find a mentor
- Be a mentor
- Have fun

Love what you do and make a living doing it.
Eat at Wahoo's Fish Taco.

Wing Lam
Founder and Co-Owner, Wahoo's Fish Taco
Wing.lam@wahoos.com

80

Don't Erase It...Embrace It!
Doug Nielsen

Have you ever had the dream where you are sitting in a school class and suddenly realize you are wearing only underwear? Most of us greatly fear looking foolish. We live our lives in a defensive mode, trying to make sure that we don't do anything that will make us seem odd, or cause others to laugh at our expense. One experience in my life has taught me a different way of living.

My eight-year-old son, Stratton, had made me promise that I would interrupt my workday to play with him. I agreed to play anything he wanted if he would wait patiently for two hours.

Exactly two hours later, Stratton informed me that he and his buddy, Matt, were ready for me to come hunt snakes with them. I immediately blurted out "No way! You know I hate snakes." He quickly replied "You promised that we could do whatever I wanted!"

I reluctantly surrendered, fervently praying that we would not see any slithering creatures. Not 10 feet outside of our house, my son gave a yelp of joy. He held up the most hideous thing I had ever seen, a ten foot rattler, about as fat as my thigh! (Actually it was a scrawny three-foot water snake, but fear magnifies). In his excitement, it slipped out of Stratton's hands and fell through the safety grate of the basement window well. I held up the grate while Stratton jumped in. The last thing I remember is hearing "I'm throwing it up." I looked down in horror, opened my mouth and said, "Don't!"

No sooner had I done that when I felt a cold, slimy, snake wrap around my neck and open mouth. In a frenzy, I gave a blood-curdling yell (more like a scream), ripped the snake off my neck, and threw it as far from me as possible.

I eventually regained my composure and began to wonder about that scream. I sensed it might not have been the most manly response. It didn't help matters when Matt said to my son, "Wow.

Your dad screams louder than my little sister."

Just as I was about to launch into an explanation that would save my reputation, I remembered the phrase my business partner, Tim, and I often use in our presentations, "Don't erase it, embrace it!" We challenge them to embrace who they are, and capitalize on their eccentricities. To attain success you must be willing to make mistakes, to be different, and stand out.

I squared my shoulders, put on a smile and said to the boys, "Do you think that snake was half as scared as I was?" Since that time, I have become the brunt of many good-natured snake jokes, and I laugh right along with them.

I have learned that I can't be happy while I fear what others will think. I love the life I live, because I have learned to love the person I am. I don't try to ERASE me, *I EMBRACE me!*

Doug Nielsen
Tim & Doug Speakers
801-391-4356
www.timanddoug.com

A Eulogy For W.C. Fields
Ronald J. Fields

I was a devoted admirer of the actor, W.C. Fields, long before I discovered I was his grandson.

Around my tenth birthday, the family had gathered in front of the television to watch a W.C. Fields film, a fairly common past time in our house. This time, *It's A Gift* was on the air. During the famous "back porch" scene and again in the "drugstore" scene with Mr. Muckle, I laughed so hard my side ached and I had to leave the room to catch my breath. My sister was concerned so she followed me out to make sure I hadn't passed out. When I caught my breath, I told her, "W.C. Fields has to be the funniest man who ever lived!"

She said, "You don't know do you?"

"Know what?" I asked.

"W.C. Fields is your grandfather," she informed me.

It came as quite a shock.

I loved his gags and his one-liners. But now I see so much more than just laughs. I see an artist at work and I see the self portrait of that artist through his films.

"To thine own self be true," was his motto. W.C. challenged every producer, director and studio head to keep his creations pure. In all his characters, surviving unsullied, were the elements human dignity and self. He fought so hard for these characterizations, that he alienated all the studios for which he worked.

When asked to advertise the film, *You Can't Cheat an Honest Man*, which would have put extra money in his own pocket, he refused. He claimed that the director edited out all elements of human kindness from his character. Thus, his advertising would be dishonest, and he would not do such a thing.

In art and in life, W.C. maintained his dignity and his integrity and because of these traits, many great writers acknowledged him. James Agee once penned that even when Fields looked Worn and Torn, he remained, As Noble as Stone Mountain.

Through his noble work, W.C. still lives. He was an honest man and everyone knows *You Can't Cheat An Honest Man.*

Ronald J. Fields
#1 Best Selling Author
Emmy Award Winning Writer
www.wcbiz.com

84

Work Yourself Happy
Terri Levine

How many people do you know who are happy in their work? When you consider the time we spend commuting, working, or talking about work, it's reasonable to expect to be happy doing whatever we do for eight, ten, or twelve hours a day. The sad truth is that most people are not happy in their jobs.

So what does "Work Yourself Happy" mean? Does it mean denying your needs and working so hard that you lose yourself in your career? Or accepting whatever job you have and learning to "grin and bear it?" Or working in a job you hate but telling yourself you're enjoying it? Emphatically, no!

Working yourself happy is coming to the realization success does not mean job burn-out, unhealthy stress, being away from the things and people you love, and not being passionate about your work. It means deciding you will no longer tolerate a life that lacks work that fully nurtures you. It means you perform incredibly at work because you enjoy it so much. It means you have a career you love and work about which you are passionate.

There are five secrets to working yourself happy:

- Accept that you must let go of the past.
- Take a close look at your previous endeavors.
- Get to know yourself really well.
- Create a destination with soul.
- Enjoy the journey.

Few of us begin our careers with the intention to do something else. After all, we've invested time and money getting to where we are. Often, it's our own misguided notion that, having put so much time and effort into a career, we must stick to it. Sometimes, the fear of disappointing our family or our attachment to a huge income keeps us trapped in a career that may once have excited us, but now drags us down.

We are proud of our achievements, and give little thought to another career. "I worked hard to get where I am. I'm proud of it. People respect me. How can I give all this up now?" we may say. Yet our true self (that part of us who knows our best interests) is screaming for a change; nagging away at our thoughts until we begin to listen.

It's not about being selfish; it's about being true to yourself— respecting yourself as you respect others. Listen to yourself, then, and recognize your needs. It's the first step towards a happier life.

Terri Levine, Best-selling Author and Speaker
Author of: *Work Yourself Happy, Stop Managing, Start Coaching!;*
Coaching For an Extraordinary Life and *Create Your Ideal Body*
www.coachinginstruction.com
www.terrilevine.com

"WHO AM I? WHY AM I?"
Don Marr

All of us are *Beings of Light* walking on a path of enlightenment. We all are just listening and looking for our place of achievement and recognition. As we look and listen for our place or niche, we think in terms of achievement or success but our true selves show up best by just being our true selves, Beings of Light and Love who share our existence and thoughts with loved ones, friends and neighbors.

Presenting our true nature of Love and Light brings out the best of us every time we experience this idea or expression. Try it. Try expressing your true nature of Loving to someone and see how that truly feels. This is our true nature.

Find someone or thing you truly Love and express this Love for them and feel this expression in the center of your body. How does this feel? Breathe into this idea or thought of Love. This is who we all are. Feel this to the very depth of your soul. This is who we all are. Breathe into this again and again. This is the Universal Truth of who we all are.

87

WHY AM I? "Why am I here?" This may be your next question. You are here because you are a unique representation of this experience of Love you just created. Only you can represent this unique creation or example of this kind of Love you just expressed. Only you can bring to this planet at this time this creation of expression for all to see and for you to feel. You are unique. We all are unique in our individual expression.

So express your uniqueness in every chance you get to express this Love and Light to yourself and to the world. We all make up the body of Universal Love and Light. We are just individual examples of this expression.

So, in conclusion, express your Love and your uniqueness in all your work, all your play, all your representations of who you are or who you think you are; every chance you have to express yourself.

Remember to state,

"I AM UNIVERSAL LOVE — I AM UNIVERSAL LIGHT."

We are all one in this expression.

Don Marr
Author/Speaker
A Gateway to Higher Consciousness;
My Father Calls Me (One Man's Way Back To GOD)
1stbooks.com
e-mail: Idealself@AOL.com

88

How Precious Life Is!
Robert G. Allen

It's now just months after I was involved in a terrible automobile accident, and I am happy to be alive. I have a deep appreciation for all of you. I'm not just happy to be alive but to know that we all have a brighter future to empower and bless so many people. I feel so much love and power from you through your cards and positive messages that I get choked up. Although we all come from many different faiths, you were all mainly saying that I'm in God's hands and your prayers are with me.

I want to encourage you even in the midst of crises in the world and in your own life. Because it's not just about making millions, which you will do as you find groups of people and bless them with your time, your money, your spirit and your positive message. You will keep going forward step by step along the path you are destined to travel so you will make the most of your life.

I'm more aware of how precious and short life is. I've never been a moody person so I didn't understand other people's moods and depressions until this accident. This was the first time that I felt that I might not pull out and recover from the accident. I congratulate you for persisting. I remember a famous singer saying after her accident that she always appreciated her fans but she didn't love them until after the accident. I appreciate and love the people that I work with more than I ever did before.

Robert G. Allen
#1 New York Times best selling author of:
Nothing Down, Multiple Streams of Income and *Creating Wealth.*
Co-author: *One Minute Millionaire*

89

90

Creative Mind
Matt Bacak

Dear Friend:

This is the true story of a 12-year old.

Raised in a small, hardworking steel town near Youngstown, Ohio, his entrepreneurial life began as he went from lemonade stand to delivering newspapers.

He was not only responsible for delivering the papers to his subscribers but also for collecting their money. This responsibility caused him to develop relationships with all of his subscribers. He got to know their families, their birthdays, and even their pets.

Two months after starting his paper route, he had an instant moneymaking idea while standing at a neighbor's door collecting. After receiving the check, he asked, "I noticed that your husband is out of town, and the grass is high. Would you like me to mow your grass for $20?" Patiently waiting, he heard his first "yes."

Incredibly, his first week he created 10 new lawn care clients from his subscribers.

The real story begins after mowing the first two lawns, he asked himself "What am I going to do? I don't have time. I have homework; I have to go to school, and I have to deliver my papers. Now, I have all these lawns to mow."

The answer came at the bus stop. His neighbor wanted money to buy baseball cards. Not only did the new entrepreneur smile, but he also solved the neighbor's problem. He told him "I have a few yards in the neighborhood that need to be mowed. Would you like to mow them? I'll pay you $5 an hour." He replied, "Yes."

The neighbor was as excited as the new entrepreneur, when he found that each yard took him only one hour. With a passive income (money you don't work for) of $15 a yard, he began his first real business. That day "Grass Busters" was born, and all he had to do was collect money.

Imagine what thinking like this 12-year old boy could do for your life! Be creative! Find a way to earn a passive income. By the way, that 12 year-old boy was me.

Warmest Regards,

Matt Bacak
The Powerful Promoter
1-866-MATT-123
www.powerfulpromoter.com

92

A Long Journey
Lodavina Grosnickle

It has been a long journey. You see, coming from a large, poor family from the Philippines, I had to start work at the age of five. I knew it was important to make a lot of money for my well-being and health. I supported myself and paid my way on my own through college.

When I was in the Philippines I helped a friend start a furniture business. We started with $350 and, now, it's a 2.5 million company. I left to go to the United States.

I was always busy in different things for many years and one day my husband said, "Enough is enough." I needed to stop my entrepreneuring and to work a regular job. Well, we were in financial difficulties at the time, but I asked for one more chance. Then, if I had to, I would go to an "8-to-5" job. And then, my daughter shook my life, too.

For the first ten years of her life I was a 100% mom. Then I started net working when she was ten and was always busy. She must have felt that I didn't have time for her anymore. I was married to my career, I always gave 110%, but I gave it to the job— not my daughter. So when she was eighteen, she moved out.

I was devastated. In the Philippines, our motto is, "Family always stays together," and I felt that I had failed as a parent to her. When she left I woke up.

Then M.S.T.G.S. came along and I knew that I could help people who were in financial difficulties. I love to help people and, if you help someone in any way, it will come back to you ten fold. I knew I could help people get back on their feet without forcing them to forget their dreams.

The lesson I have learned from my business experience is that you can have many things in life. You don't have to settle for what others think you should. You have worth and value. You can

93

achieve the income you want. Money is not everything, but making money allows you the time to spend with your family and to realize your dreams. Now I can travel anywhere I want and spend quality time with my family. I appreciate the little things in life. One day my husband was mowing the lawn and I was in the kitchen watching out the window and saw all the pretty rose bushes he had planted and I thanked him for all of the flowers I get every day. It's the little things in life that mean the most and are appreciated.

I tell my clients, "Keep dreaming and never give up." There are many failures in life but it's not how much you fail, it's how many times you pick yourself back up! Always be at peace, with God and with your family.

Gorgeous Ludy Grosnickle.
M.S.T.G Solutions
www.gorgeousludy.us
ludyg2002@yahoo.com

94

Spiritual Life: The Tragedy of The Unasked Question
Reverend Doctor Symeon Rodger

A wise man once asked his disciple "What is the greatest tragedy of human life?" "Not finding the answers you're looking for?" asked the disciple. "No," replied the sage, "It is failing to ask the questions in the first place."

There is a lot of talk these days about spiritual life. It is astounding that so few of us ask, *"What is spiritual life?"*

If we reflect on the world's great spiritual traditions, we conclude that the essence of spiritual life revolves around refining the quality and direction of our thoughts. Our thoughts have a tremendous impact on both our emotional and physical wellbeing.

The next obvious question we seldom ask is: *"So then, how important is spiritual life; where does it rank among my many competing priorities?"*

Every tradition says that our spiritual life is critical to our fate beyond the grave. In addition, the latest medical research provides conclusive proof that spiritual life is among the most important determining factors in happiness and longevity. It is clear that we should probably consider giving spiritual life "top billing."

If spiritual life is so critical, then we next have to ask: *"What does it take to be successful in spiritual life?"*

It is a paradox of human existence that spirituality has fewer serious students than any other endeavor though it is considered to be of greatest importance. If we ran our businesses as carelessly as we run our spiritual lives, we would undoubtedly be in bankruptcy court.

To become successful in any field, it is necessary to follow in the footsteps of someone who has succeeded. This is an unbreakable universal law. If you follow the path of another person and train the way another person trains, you will inevitably see similar results.

To search for a successful mentor, however, implies that you

95

already know the desired results. If you do, you are most unusual. **What's astonishing is not just that people do not know what they *should* be looking for, but that they seldom have a clear idea of what they *are* looking for.**

Here on planet Earth we have real spiritual traditions and false ones. The authentic traditions have detailed methods for training the mind. They have living lineages of spiritual fathers and mothers. They demonstrate that in every age and time their methods have produced people full of perfect, selfless love who have gone beyond the laws of time and space. False traditions simply teach you how to be a nice person. If you're clever, you'll probably realize you can do that on your own without their help!

Your success in life depends on your spiritual life, which in turn depends on asking the right questions and being brutally honest in your answers.

Two things are imperative: first, your spiritual life aims must be correct. Aiming in the wrong direction will leave you unfulfilled or perhaps place you in harm's way. Second, the methodology and training must be correct. Nothing happens in life without diligent training, but the wrong training methods will also take you to the wrong objective.

Ask! Think! Examine! Question everything! *Don't let your precious life become a tragedy of unasked questions.*

Reverend Doctor Symeon Rodger
Orthodox Church in America
www.symeonrodger.com

Why I am happy to be living life
Dr. Linnda Durré

Many things have allowed me to live a happy life.

First, my family. My family was large, my father being one of nine children. All were generous, loving and full of boisterous energy. I spent the majority of my early childhood surrounded by family in a large house that I shared with my parents, grandparents and uncles. It provided a very safe and secure feeling. On Sunday, it was tradition for family and friends to gather for dinner.

I went through a very transitional time at the age of four. Not only was I kicked off the "only child" pedestal when my little sister Lois was born, but I also had to cope with the loss of my grandfather. After his death, our family continued to live in that house for two years but moved soon after I turned six to a town six miles away.

I credit my mother, Catherine, with her unconditional love, nurturance, warmth, and belief that I could do and be anything. My father, Theodore, made Lou Gossett in "An Officer and A Gentleman," look like Richard Simmons. He gave me the focus, discipline and drive that channeled my natural tenacity, insatiable curiosity, and high energy to succeed in all I do, which was fueled by my desire to earn his love and approval.

I've followed Mark Twain's advice: "Find work you love, and you'll never work a day in your life." I do so many things that I love; I'm always busy and constantly challenging myself. Knowing I've contributed positively to people's lives and to the planet, makes me sleep soundly.

As a psychotherapist for 25 years, I've assisted people dealing with everything life throws at you. I've been through tough times, too, when I've learned powerful lessons about humility, ego, and hubris, which have deepened my appreciation for my faith, family, and friends. My belief in God faltered many times over the years, but God's faith in me was relentless.

Happiness is a choice — a conscious decision to believe in yourself and in God which is an unbeatable combination!

Linnda Durré, Ph.D.
Dreams Come True Enterprises, LLC
127 West Fairbanks Avenue, #501
Winter Park, FL 32789
Cell (407) 739-8620
Phone (407) 246-4681
Fax (407) 599-7780
Pager (407) 228-2946

98

Inner Directed Marketing:
A New Way to Prosper in Tough Times
Joe Vitale

More and more people today are beginning to realize that their power for creating wealth in the world and living the life they love isn't THEIR power at all. Instead, it's the right use of THE power—which is the energy of all that is.

But, how do you tap into this power?

Simple. I call it "Inner Directed Marketing." Consider it a shorthand version of the steps in my book, "Spiritual Marketing."

Here's how it works:

Step One: Set an intention.

Intention rules the earth. When you state "I WILL..." or "I AM..." and then complete the sentence with a clear statement of whatever it is you want to be, do, or have, you create a command that vibrates with power. An example might be, "I WILL write an article on Inner Directed Marketing that helps people easily get better results and which will somehow lead to my receiving $50,000 every month in passive income."

Tall order? Maybe. But I believe anything is possible, so why not shoot for the moon? As Robert Collier said, "Plant the seed of desire in your mind and it forms a nucleus with power to attract to itself everything needed for its fulfillment."

Step Two: Let it go.

Letting go is where the magic happens. Letting go means that you will be fine if you get your intention AND you will be fine you don't get it. It's a state of cool detachment. It's a state of neutrality toward your intention: You WANT it but you don't NEED it. When you release your intention to the world, you are releasing a "magic spell" that will stir the energy of all that is to do your bidding.

Now, this doesn't mean you don't DO anything. Instead, what

it means is you act on the impulses you get and the opportunities you receive. By doing so, you'll be brought to the thing you want—or to something even better.

Does this inside-out approach to living the life of your dreams actually work?

You bet. I have over a dozen popular books out now, several best-sellers, several audiotapes, a best-selling audio program with Nightingale-Conant, a country estate, a second home, a luxury sports car, and much more. I am living my dream. Ahh, yes!

I've always felt there was an escalator through life. I've found it. And I just showed you where it is.

Won't you step up and enjoy the ride?

Joe Vitale
Author of *Spiritual Marketing, Hypnotic Writing,*
The Power of Outrageous Marketing,
Adventures Within: Confessions of an Inner World Journalist.
www.mrfire.com

100

Shine Bright
Jill Lublin

To live the life you love, you must first love the life you live! It is important to love where you are right now. It is perfect for who you are right now. I notice, in living the life I love, that it is a life filled with connecting with others; with love, travel, friends, kindness, service, and enjoying nature. It includes quiet time on the deck, playing with my cats, reading, and doing work I'm passionate about.

I start each day with prayer. I light a candle each morning and turn on my fountain. I write three high value activities I will focus on that day in order to meet my monthly goals. I schedule my time, but I allow time for flexibility too. Still, time is scheduled for sales calls, clients, exercise, dates, and unstructured time—time to get up and do whatever I want!

I focus on results for my clients. In that commitment I have found tremendous freedom. I live as fully present in each moment as possible. Each morning, I go out to my deck and turn around in a circle and look at all the possibilities.

It is important to emanate great energy and focus on the possibilities. What we focus on grows! It is so important to stay positive and to look forward, no matter how the circumstances may appear at the moment. The circumstances will change, but your focus – your dreams and your commitment to a better tomorrow – will be a constant. Nurture your spirit, whatever that means to you. Love yourself more. Love others more, and do more acts of kindness for others. Who we are to each other

101

and who we are to ourselves makes all the difference. It makes us shine in a world that is, for some, a dark place.

Let your lights shine bright.

Jill Lublin, CEO
Promising Promotion
Author, National Best-Seller *Guerrilla Publicity*
Syndicated Radio Host, *Do The Dream*
(415) 883-5455
www.promisingpromotion.com
jill@planetlink.com

102

Health Care to Wealth Care™
Dr. J. D. Clement

Imagine waking up every morning and doing exactly what you want to do, living as if everyday was the weekend. That's my life: the weekend, all week long. It wasn't always this way. I used to have jobs with bosses, deadlines, budget meetings, and cut-backs. I decided to stop working and start living a fuller life.

I am living the life of my dreams because I implemented a plan to do exactly that. Many people have great plans to pursue their life's dream but never get around to implementing it. It's like planning a farm crop but never planting the seeds. Without planting the crop, there's nothing to eat. My mindset became one of abundance as I focused on building my financial foundation.

I've dedicated 16 years to becoming financially literate after discovering the hard way that financial literacy is not generally taught, not even professional schools like medical school.

When I graduated from medical school, I had a 25-year payback schedule for massive school loans and found quickly that, despite everything I learned, medical school did not equip me with the financial skills I needed to manage this heavy burden. So I dedicated myself to learning wealth care just as I had learned health care. Thankfully, I was able to develop a plan that allowed me to pay off my student loans ten years early.

I am now living the life of my dreams and continue to find more and varied opportunities. My perspective is open to abundance in all aspects of my life. I have more time to spend with family and friends, more time to grow personally, and more time to volunteer with organizations like Freedom From Hunger (**www.freedomfromhunger.org**) where you can truly make a difference in someone's life. I have more time to travel the world

103

to experience a variety of cultures and languages.

Learning how to care for your wealth will help you live the life of your dreams. Don't wait! Start living today!

J. Denise Clement, M.D.
International author, speaker, physician, entrepreneur, filmmaker
info@healthcaretowealthcare.com
www.healthcaretowealthcare.com

104

You Are the Enterprise
William K. Ellermeyer

Have you noticed the dramatic changes in the working world over the past two decades? The days of paternalistic corporations providing job stability and extensive benefit programs are quickly becoming a part of the past. Professional work has downsized to become short-term projects, with a beginning and an end averaging about 18 to 36 months. No longer can individuals rely on a corporation to "take care of them." In a very real way...
We are all Self-employed.

The increasing fact of business life is that we are in transition throughout our lives with the possibility of multiple careers: 10 to 20 jobs over the course of a working life. The rapidity of change is unprecedented, making it clear we are living in one of the most dynamic periods of modern industrial history.

The first step is to understand that you are a free agent, choosing to use your skills in a traditional job or perhaps working for yourself by deploying your skills over multiple streams of income. Let's say your skills and experience are in marketing. You could start a consultancy in marketing, get a part-time job two days a week working as director of marketing for a small company, teach a course in marketing at a local college or university, or get on the board of a small company that needs marketing know-how.

You need to be the captain of your own ship. This will allow you to integrate work and living to achieve a work/life balance — something most people are seeking but few achieve.

Think of yourself as the business. Brainstorm all the ways you can create the income to make a living. You may have an undiscovered business within you, or the desire to buy a small business that is consistent with your passions, skills and interests. The secret is to discover your unique skills by going back through your life and analyzing your successes. Where do your passions lie?

For your free gift, go to: **www.wakeupand.com**

When have you accomplished great things? Find your inherent skills and apply them!

Remember, there are very few career ladders remaining out there. If you are not earning more or learning more, it's time to give yourself a promotion by moving on to something new.

Remember: *you **are** the enterprise!*

William K. Ellermeyer
Career Coach, Irvine CA
949-786-5490
elosman@aol.com

106

Hanging by a String
Marilyn Gibson

For as long as I can remember, music has been a part of my life. Until the age of 16, my violin practice was sporadic. It was then that I had a vision. I remember watching the room transform into blue sky with tumbling silver clouds. I had an overwhelming feeling of bliss and peace. I heard pure sounds and perfect harmonies. Music had unlocked a heavenly gate, which had transported me beyond the dimensions of reality.

As I reflected on this vision, I knew that it was my destiny was to become a professional violinist. My playing went from sporadic to constant. I practiced diligently and, as a result of my self-discipline, I was awarded a college scholarship to play violin.

Everything was going well until one day, as I was taking my violin out of the case, I noticed that the two middle joints of my playing fingers were swollen. My greatest fear was confirmed—I had lupus.

107

Being diagnosed with lupus was disappointing but not shocking; my mother died from complications with lupus. I experienced flares and tried to cure it through natural means but ended up becoming weaker and weaker. Barely able to function, I finally dragged myself to a hospital emergency room where I had a near-death experience.

I remember seeing a glowing golden tunnel before me. In it stood a smiling man dressed in a splendid robe. Brilliant white light radiated from his being. I sensed a gentleness in him but an incredible power as well. This was my Master, leading me into this glorious tunnel.

As I was being guided toward the tunnel, something pulled me back. On the third morning of my stay at the emergency room, I awoke, ready to begin a new life. I put my hands together in thanks, realizing that the Earth was once again my home.

I returned to my violin with a new perspective on life, but that didn't control the flares that were causing the lupus to attack my kidneys. Once again I was admitted to the hospital. Although I was put on dialysis, I successfully overcame the flares through prayer, affirmation, and visualization. For eight and a half months I was healthy. Unfortunately, my kidneys reverted causing me to go back on dialysis. Instead of waiting patiently for them to improve once again, my father donated his kidney. The transplant not only saved my life but it also prevented my father from losing another loved one to lupus.

Now, 12 years later, I am in excellent condition. Gratitude, faith and humor helped me to recover and they also help me lead a fulfilling life today. Lupus-free, I play in Carnegie Hall, Lincoln Center and on Broadway, and with my piano trio, The Herrick Trio.

This poem describes my life journey:

Begin   *Setting aside the trials*   *of Yesterday,*

Pushing away the fears   *for Tomorrow,*

I walk the straight and   *narrow path*   *of Today.*

Not easy,   *yet the simplest*   *of all things.*

Strive without strife,   *Love without self,*

Be without fear,   *ever being retaught.*

When all that is required   *is*   *to*   ***Begin.***

Marilyn Gibson
www.hangingbyastring.com
1-800-441-8786.

108

LIVE THE LIFE YOU LOVE

Safe and Sound
Marlene Coleman, MD

A family vacation is valuable opportunity to enjoy quality time together. Traveling with children—even one child—involves preparation/challenges rarely experienced by adults traveling alone.

As a physician for over 25 years with a special interest in family travel, I often advise families to discover the benefits of travel. With realistic expectations and thoughtful planning, every vacation can be exciting, fulfilling, and relaxing for the entire family. It can also provide excellent relief from the stresses of the daily hustle and bustle. My passion for this topic has led to the writing of Safe and Sound, Healthy Travel with Children.

Healthy travel involves more than just the prevention of disease and physical injury. It also incorporates mental and emotional well-being. As a family approaches their adventure, Travelers should keep the following in mind:

- Remind yourself who gives your life meaning.
- Be open and willing to discover new passions.
- Experience the excitement of meeting new people.
- Dispel misconceptions you may have regarding other cultures and people.
- Feel personal power by experiencing exciting and different cultures.
- Cure that "trapped" feeling.
- Enhance your sense of independence and confidence.
- Engage in new topics of conversation to share with others.
- Allow yourself time to be pampered and to relax.
- Explore your feelings and open your soul to personal enlightenment.

If you're considering a journey, consider why you are going

109

before deciding where. Examine your thoughts, concerns, and dreams about travel. Keep a "wish list" of things you want to experience. Keep your imagination open, share your ideas with those you love, and then have the adventure of a lifetime.

Bon Voyage!

Marlene Coleman, MD
Author of: *Safe and Sound: Healthy Travel With Children*
Mcsafeandsound@earthlink.net

110

LIVE THE LIFE YOU LOVE

They All Thought I Was Crazy…
Until The $2.1 Million Bid Came In
Donald Peters

Striking out on your own can make you seem crazy to your family, friends and co-workers. I always wanted to have my own business and was even making a real estate investment on the day I was laid-off from a six-figure income position. It came at the worst time for me, my wife was seven months pregnant, we just bought a big (spelled expensive) truck, and the economy was on a downward spiral.

After four months of being unemployed I started selling my personal belongings on *eBay* out of desperation to survive. I was pretty successful at selling items and thought "I could sell other peoples things for them also."

Low and behold, *IwillSELLyourSTUFF.com* was born and I was in business. The very next week I started handing out business cards and telling everyone *"I will sell your stuff on eBay."*

The following week I ended up with two contracts and an excellent start for my fledgling company. I realized that it was fairly easy to find other peoples' stuff to sell. Most know nothing about selling on the Internet, and that is where I could step in. The challenge would be actually making the sale.

I landed a contract for a Missile Silohome that ended after a month with no bids. At this point all my relatives and friends were skeptical that I could sell anything and that this crazy idea of selling on eBay was a pipe dream. I knew that someone out there was willing to buy this Silohome—I just had to find the right person and I eventually did.

My business is now focused on high-dollar and very unusual items. I have since sold a few 727 Airplane Homes and typically have unusual items for sale like Inflatable Churches, Personal

111

Bunkers, Private Islands, and I once even sold The Millionaire Mentor!

No longer am I required to punch a clock and put in eight hours knowing that I could do the work in two. Working at home is an awesome experience. I followed the advice *"when you are ready to quit, take one more step forward."* You know, striking out on your own can sometimes be crazy good.

Donald L. Peters
210-541-8374
don@IwillSELLyourSTUFF.com
www.IwillSELLyourSTUFF.com
www.AirplaneHomes.com

112

Dreams Become Reality
Dr. K. J. Ogden

The first light of dawn glistens on the mountains. The waves crash on the sand. No, it's not a dream! It's reality.

My laptop screen saver shows a person with a computer in her lap, her feet propped on a banister with her gaze reflecting first on a beautiful mountain scape, then blurring into the Sydney Opera House, vanishing to the orange red dessert sand and finally the reflection of the deep beautiful blue ocean peers back at her. This screen saver represents to me a person who is truly living her dream.

Don't get me wrong; there's nothing wrong with a "9 to 5 job," a daily routine, and the tug of life's responsibilities at your sleeve. But why live that life when, through modern technology, I can live my dream of freedom? My laptop hooks to my cell phone which connects to the satellite that beams me to the Internet. I'm set to conquer the world from any point in space or time!

The only connection to a physical reality is that the dog still needs to be walked. As I gaze out at the pounding waves I notice a car pulled to the side of the road. Three eager people jump out and race down the sand and squeal as the waves wash over their feet. I wasn't sure if they were thrilled with the first light of dawn and that first step into the pacific or if it was just so cold they were surprised. For whatever reason, I was here to enjoy it with them instead of traveling on the Los Angeles freeways listening to honking horns, seeing brake lights and wondering why I take on this traffic day after day.

Life is too short to end the race and think, "what if?" What if I hadn't given up? What if I'd dared to live my dream? What if I had taken one more step?

A school of dolphins swims by. Several babies are learning to

113

jump. It reminds me that we all must learn to take that first leap if we will live our dreams.

Dr. K. J. Ogden
President & CEO
Soaring Eagle Visions Inc
818-772-1062; 800-903-6066
Soaring High and Free
www.3StepsToSuccess.com

114

Painfully Blessed
Rich Bella

Many of us juggle a schedule of work, work, and more work. We get so caught up in the routine of our daily lives that we neglect to realize the blessings we have taken advantage of for so long. Some blessings are huge, while others might not be so obvious until we try to get by without them.

About six weeks before the birth of my second daughter Jada, I was picking up my 22-month-old daughter Jordin to put her in the car seat. As I lifted her, I pulled my left shoulder. The pain was so intense that all I could do was sit completely still in the back seat with Jordin. I held my shoulder, hoping the pain would subside but there was no relief.. After a few minutes, Jordin looked at me and asked, "Are you okay?" I said, "No, babe. Daddy's hurt."

Two weeks passed and the pain persisted. I was medicating with all sorts of over-the-counter pain relievers in search of some kind of help. The pain subsided but only for four hours at a time. The pain was relentless and I was worried that it would restrict my range of motion and cause me to get out of shape. Even cardiovascular exercise that required little shoulder movement caused pain. Everything I was used to doing was no longer an easy task. It was painful, it was difficult, and it was tiring. For as frustrating as this injury was, I was humbled by the hard lesson I was learning.

I decided to research a particular yoga class to see if that would remedy the injury. It did. Ever since I walked into a Bikram yoga studio my life has changed dramatically. For anyone who has taken Bikram yoga, or any other type of disciplined martial arts knows the meaning of humility. The instructors acknowledged the severity of my shoulder injury, a pulled levator scapula. Although they were aware of the severity of the injury, they did not pity me. Instead, they

115

pushed me and expected more than I thought I could handle.

Part of what makes Bikram yoga so beneficial is that the room is heated to 103 degrees, immediately warming the body which is excellent for stretching and healing. After my first class, it was obvious that my condition was improving. I continue to go to yoga today not only to maintain the improved condition of my shoulder but also to remind me that the mind is an essential ingredient in healing the body. I learned the importance of concentrating on my breathing and releasing tension from the mind through the body while strengthening my spirit. The healing of my body helped me to focus on what was really important in my life. For the first time in a long time, I was not concerned about a business plan, road map, or marketing strategy. I was more preoccupied with the blessings I have been given in my life; a wonderful wife, two beautiful daughters, a sharp mind and a resilient body. Now, I am truly living a life I love.

Rich Bella
Business Owner/ Fitness Expert
www.rasetraining.com
866-435-8003

116

Picasso of the Sea
Wyland

Many years ago, while visiting friends at the Dolphin Research Center in the Florida Keys, the Director, Mandy Rodrigues, asked if I would like to paint with some of the dolphins. Of course, I wondered how this was going to work. I made my way to a lagoon where, to my surprise, a small group of bottlenose dolphins greeted me with excitement.

As I sat on the edge of the dock and readied my water-based acrylic paints, the dolphins became even more excited. I, too, was excited about collaborating with these highly intelligent mammals of the deep. If any animal on earth (besides humans) could create a work of art, it most certainly would be dolphins.

I passed a paintbrush to a dolphin named Kibby, who took the handle in her mouth. Next I held up a canvas and she began immediately to paint in the style of Picasso, laying down each stroke with a twist of her head and, finally, with a 360-degree spin. When she was done she passed the brush back to me and watched as I painted my part.

As two very diverse marine artists, Kibby and I shared a single canvas. But discovered that we also shared something else—tears of joy. Together we had created something uniquely beautiful; a one-of-a-kind collaboration between two artists of two completely different worlds.

Later, I told my friends on the dock that it was just the salt that made my eyes water. But they knew it was the feeling I had for my newfound friend of the sea.

When the painting was finished, Kibby smiled a big dolphin grin. She nodded her head in approval of the completed work, then lifted her flukes above the surface and dived below. A few

117

seconds later she brought me the highest honor a dolphin can give: a gift from the sea. It was a rock!

There are wonders in this world; wonders of which we haven't dreamed. Seek new places; find new friends, and wonder with me.

Wyland: Artist of the sea
www.wyland.com

118

My Mission

R. Winn Henderson, M.D.

I opened my eyes and looked around. All I could see was concrete—stark, white concrete. I was locked up in a concrete cage. I counted my possessions. I had 13 things: my clothing, toiletries, and my Bible. In spite of these miserable conditions, I was happy; happier than before when I was a medical doctor earning $50,000 a month and had all the "things" a person could want.

I know this statement is hard to believe, but let me share my experience.

I was in shock; I found myself in a federal holding cell after a trial gone terribly wrong. What was going on? Why was I here? How could a mistake like this be made? I felt like Daniel in the lion's den. I cried out to God to tell me why.

The next part of my journey began with a prophecy (the foretelling of a future event based on divine inspiration). I went to sleep, and during the night, God spoke to me in a dream.

God said that the reason I found myself in this position was because He had a message He wanted to be delivered. He promised me three things. First, like Daniel, no harm would come to me. Second, He would provide everything I needed to accomplish this task. Finally, when the task was accomplished, I would be released. I truly believed that this was a holy prophecy. Almost everyone who heard my story thought I was nuts. It didn't matter to me; I believed.

For two years I worked on the book God told me to write. I was kept safe. He provided everything I needed, including $5,000 to print the book. One day at mail call, the first copy of the book arrived to me in prison. I quickly reviewed it. Everything God had told me to relay was there.

Then, God fulfilled the last part of His promise. Exactly 40 hours after I had the book in my hands, prison officials came and got me, put me on a plane, and sent me home.

119

LIVE THE LIFE YOU LOVE

Through this experience, God showed me that each of us is very special to Him. We are His children. He created each of us with a purpose. If we will find that purpose (our destiny) and pursue it, we will be happy, content, and have peace of mind beyond under-standing. My mission— to spread this message.

R. Winn Henderson, M.D.
International Radio Talk Show Host of *Share Your Mission,*
Author of 13 Books, and founder of The Destiny House.
To receive one of his books for free: e-mail your request to
dhenderson7 @mchsi.com.
More information is available at:
www.theultimatesecrettohappiness.com

120

Enthusiasm
Cynthia Kersey

Without a doubt, enthusiasm has contributed greatly to my accomplishments. It has been my experience that a positive attitude not only benefits you but is also contagious, spreading passion and excitement to those around us.

Enthusiasm provides the energy to overcome any obstacle and the rewards are immediate:

You'll be highly motivated

Enthusiasm is the fuel that drives you. It is an inexhaustible resource for energy and optimism.

Work will seem like play

Enthusiastic people find it difficult to use the word 'work.' Such people are pursuing what they most enjoy and what is personally rewarding.

Others will share your passion and enthusiasm

Enthusiasm draws like a magnet, attracting others to your cause. Sometimes other people are not even sure why they've joined up. Their logic tells them 'no,' yet instinctively they say 'yes.' Nothing sells like enthusiasm and passion!

Imagine how much richer your life could be if you injected enthusiasm on a daily basis. Choosing activities that align with your purpose and support your strengths will cause passion to follow automatically. You will begin to approach each day with wonder, joy, and expectation.

Find what you love and give yourself to it completely. Having done this, you will become unstoppable.

Cynthia Kersey
Best-selling author of "Unstoppable"
www.Unstoppable.net

121

122

Create a Life You Love
And Help Your Kids Do The Same!
Pam Ragland

"We are what we repeatedly do. Excellence then is not an act, but a habit." Aristotle.

Are you a singer? Artist? Well, ask any four-year old if they are a singer or an artist, and the answer is a resounding "Yes!" So, what happens when we become adults? Why do we decide we can't do things? Why don't we believe the truth—*we can do absolutely anything we decide to do?"*

We create our current reality based on the exact words we think. We all have negative "thought habits" which we adopted very early in our little lives from those nearest and dearest to us. We accepted those negative beliefs—and words—about why we can't do some-thing. They run in the background of our lives, creating our life by habit. If you think, "I am shy" you will be shy! It's that simple. We don't even realize they are there—*yet they control us.*

123

Children copy us—positively or negatively. Most thought habits started with our parents, who learned from their parents. If you want your children to live a life they love, *break the pattern by creating positive thought habits in your children.* Help them be so full of self-esteem they can't help but create a life they love!

- **Heed your words**—*Thought habits start with the first words children hear.* Say, "You're so smart." and children will say that to themselves—and create it in their lives.
- **Guide your children's words**—Help them to use words that are positive and personal ("I am…"), and reflect what they want to achieve.
- **Listen to your children**—Don't talk at or over them. *Talking to them helps them feel valued.*
- **Keep it positive**—Instead of "Don't do X" say "Do Y." *The mind creates in the positive.*

For your free gift, go to: **www.wakeupand.com**

- ☒ **Catch them doing things right**—Look for things your kids do right, and praise that. *You get more of what you reward.*
- ☒ **Focus on the behavior, don't label the child**—*Labels become thought habits.* Instead of "Bad boy," say, "Love your sister."
- ☒ **Always love your children**—no matter what! *Self-esteem is a bi-product of unconditional love.* It's a huge gift to give children so much love; they have a surplus of love to give back to the world.
- ☒ **You are always teaching**—Every word, every action teaches something. Ask yourself *"What am I teaching now?"*

"We ask ourselves,
'Who am I to be brilliant, gorgeous, talented, and fabulous?'
Actually, who are you not to be?" Nelson Mandela

Pam Ragland
President and Founder of Aiming Higher Success Coaching
Pam@AimingHigher.com
www.AimingHigher.com
949-713-7303

Dreams are Everything
Smiljan Mori

I remember a time when I was 7 years old. I set a goal that I would help other people. I didn't have a clue what I would do, but I had the deep desire to help. Maybe it was because my Dad was a musician; when he was entertaining people, they were happy. I thought, "I could do something like that."

But years showed that I didn't have the talent for music. So I set another goal: to become a policeman. Policemen, I thought, were there to help other people. So the police academy was a very good choice for me, because my parents didn't have the money to support my education and the police academy paid for everything.

But I soon realized that police work was not for me. My position was secure, but there was no opportunity for growth. There were limits, and I wanted opportunity. So one day I made the decision to give up security. I understood my reasons, but it was difficult for others to share my desire; when I left the police, my parents kicked me out of the house.

So there I was with a good education, but no money in my pocket, no entrepreneurial skills, and no knowledge about business. But I dreamed about having my own business. I started to sell life insurance to anyone I met. I had a strong vision of the future and I was very happy. I was helping people.

I was training my sales agents well and, after three years of struggle, my organization was one of the top companies in the industry. During these three years, I was listening to audiotapes and reading books. I put all of my money into my education and, because my goal was to inspire more people, I started another business. In one year, it was the top company in the training field.

There I was, a no-name guy, and I had produced the first personal growth seminars in Solvenia.

125

For your free gift, go to: www.wakeupand.com

People are always asking me, "How did you succeed overnight?" I tell them, "It was easy, but the night was 5 years long!"

Look: if I made it, you can too. You must have a vision, but remember:

A vision without motivation is nothing

A motivation without action is just a dream

But a vision with *"motivaction"* can change the world

Smiljan Mori
Best selling author of: *7 Secrets to Motivaction*
www.smiljanmori.com

126

Live the Life You Have
John Russell

What if I did not wake up one day? Would I have been accomplished? Did I achieve everything I had set out to do? Did I make the world a better place for mankind, my family and myself? When I wake up in the morning or from a nap, do I live my dreams? Or do I simply conform to society and do the minimum to succeed. Do I strive to be the best I can be and push myself to be the best at what I do?

Some people tell me I'm too intense and my expectations are too high. Does this make me wrong? Or make them lazy?

Striving to make my way in this world, what price am I willing to pay? Time is limited, days are short, and kids grow too fast. My friends and family are a gift—not an inconvenience. In order to achieve and build my kingdom they pay the price. What price do they pay for my success? What price do they pay for my failure? Right or wrong, success or failure, they are a part of my world. With my two hands if I don't succeed they bare the burden of my failure. With my two hands they reap the harvest of my success.

Do I play it safe and reflect on what might have been? Do I tell my kids that I have no regrets? What do I tell my kids when I think they are taking a step into the unknown? After all, I'm not a good example of "playing it safe". I've lived in such a way that security and the perks of corporate living were not appealing. I've lived my life my way. When the day comes that my kids are old enough and need to spread their wings, I will let them fly and feel the freedom of being free.

When the time comes that I don't wake up, I want my legacy to be that I was someone that did not settle for being average. I simply did not settle. I pushed the envelope of my

127

For your free gift, go to: **www.wakeupand.com**

industry and made it better. I was a better father, a superior husband and a craftsman in my field. I was someone that was a phone call away, a helping hand, and a light during someone's darkest hour.

When the day comes that I don't wake up, people will know that when I did wake up, I lived the life I had.

John Russell
Published Fitness Author
Certified Personal Fitness Trainer
Certified Kickboxing Instructor
Owner of Fittrainer1on1
www.fittrainer1on1.com
email: john@fittrainer1on1.com

128

Feel the Fire of YOUR Passion—and LIVE IT!

Mary Emmens Mazzullo

Feel your passion! Find a need to fulfill! Realize your passion and fire up your life! Passion struck me in the heart and soul and held on, as I stepped into the plane leaving Bermuda. My husband and I had treated two friends to their dream get-away wedding. That glorious day in Bermuda, I marveled, "We can't possibly be the only 4 people on the east coast, looking for a spiritual alternative to being married at a courthouse, or traditional church." It was illuminatingly obvious to me that I was meant to provide that unique atmosphere for non-traditional weddings.

Enthusiasm consumed every fiber of my being. Scribbling ideas, thoughts and questions, my fingers couldn't keep up with the ideas my brain was throwing at me. Consequently, by the time we arrived in Maryland, I could barely sit still. Abandoning my suitcase on the front porch, I zoomed off to find the perfect location for a Wedding Chapel! Impulsive? Yes. Fruitful pursuit? No!

Diligent, concerted information-seeking effort regarding wedding chapels ensued. I gathered ideas to adapt to our coastal location. Ocean weddings beckoned undeniably.

The Atlantic Ocean for magnificent sunrises; a restaurant overlooking glorious sunsets with a tropical wedding arbor there, then add a private wedding beach. Tropical wedding celebrations! Ocean City, Maryland is now the premier Destination Weddings location on the East Coast.

Visualizing success is ongoing; feng shui flags, cloth pinwheels spinning a path in the sand, seashells instead of rose petals, fresh leis from Hawaii—whatever an imagination can create.

Listening to each couple's dreams keeps us in demand. More importantly, loving others feeds our spirit. We spend our days on the beach with happy people!

129

WAKE UP... LIVE THE LIFE YOU LOVE

Now, let me ask you a personal question—what is your passion, and what are you willing to do to fuel that fire? What dream can you visualize into reality? Please e-mail me with any questions you may have about this story or the fire in your soul.

SEE YOU IN OCEAN CITY!

Mary E. Mazzullo
Pastor~Photographer~Writer~Entrepreneur
Facilitator of Personal and Financial Growth
www.OceanCityWeddings.com
www.YourFreeAgentPath.com
mmazzullo@YourFreeAgentPath.com

130

The Most Important Difference
Eric Figueroa

We live in a world that is moving faster than ever. Sometimes this pace can make us feel insignificant, but that does not prevent us from making a difference in this world.

Over the last year, I've often asked myself, "How can I make a difference? How can I impact someone's life? How can I change things?" After talking with a great friend, I realized that I was already making the most important difference.

I am a divorced father of two beautiful children, a 12 and 14 year-old. There is nothing that I cherish more in this world. Although I faced challenges, I made a commitment that, no matter what was happening in my life, I would place them first. I refused to be negative and bitter and burden them with adult worries. I remained positive, a lesson I learned from my mother. I'm not perfect but take pride in being a devoted father.

I spend time with my kids, Erika and Zachary, and not only talk to them, but listen to them and laugh with them as well. They know they can come to me for anything and that they are the two most important people in my life. I attend their school functions, sporting events and other activities. I tell them how proud I am of them and at times, can even embarrass them with my affection.

It is inevitable that parents make mistakes along the way, but if our kids know they're precious to us, there is a strong chance that they will grow into excellent adults. The opening line to Whitney Houston's "The Greatest Love of All" is: "I believe the children are the future, teach them well and let them lead the way—show them all the beauty they possess inside." It's true! The children we raise today will raise our grandchildren.

God has given us these beautiful gifts, allowing us to create an incredible cycle of good that will be realized by generations to

131

come. It starts with how we teach our children and the time we spend with them. Yes, we can make a difference! Parents are powerful creators of the future. It is our obligation to appreciate this power. By making a difference in the life of a child, you'll not only better your life, but the lives of many others—today and tomorrow. *You can touch the world!*

Eric Figueroa, Father/Author
Ericfig2000@yahoo.com

Not Far From the Tree
Mike Bernstein

There's an old adage that says, "The apple doesn't fall far from the tree." It reminds us that children are usually very similar to their parents.

But it doesn't account for apple trees that show up in foreign countries, does it? Sometimes the seed travels far before it bears fruit. But no matter what journey you may take, your roots lie in your childhood and in the things you love most.

My father owned several businesses, and one was a country club. So, I started young, playing tennis. I was able to attend the top tennis camps in the world, and I experienced a world of fitness and exercise. Health and activity became a part of my being. But at the same time, I became familiar with service businesses that featured memberships and a "club" atmosphere.

I was able to travel throughout the world, and dealing with other people gave me a well-rounded view of business and people. Whether it was a safari in Africa, or a trip through the old capitols of Europe, each experience brought lessons in life.

Studies in business in college led to an early career in sales for a health club. I moved easily into management because of my ability to work with people. I have always liked that environment, and my "good people skills" and respect for others made me a natural in customer service.

So, here's the bottom line: find an avenue that you enjoy; one that has a direct relationship to success in your field. I loved interacting with people. That helped me be a success in the sales and management of the business. If you find what you love to do and go about making it a career, you will succeed.

If you love something, it is much easier to be successful and dedicated to it. Because I enjoyed my chosen field, I was good at it. I got my experience in management at other clubs, but I always

135

knew that I wanted to own my own club. The achievement of that dream has given me a balance in life and the time to help raise my children and spend wonderful time with my family.

It's all because we stay close to our dreams. They can follow wherever you go and will lead you to where you want to be.

Mike Bernstein
Health Club Owner
mbthebern@aol.com

134

Transcend Through Divorce!
Lori Rubenstein

I have a very clear picture of myself, scrunched up in a ball on my kitchen floor, squeezed into the corner, with my hundred-pound German Shepard, Schuyler, licking my tears with his gentle tongue. I was contemplating ending it all. How I could possibly live another day? My "perfect marriage" was over. I could not have felt lower. I had discovered that my husband was sleeping with other women and spending inordinate amounts of money that we did not have. I was terrified that I could not raise and support my children alone.

I had just left a secure job with insurance, a regular paycheck and benefits to start my own business. From the outside, I was very together and extremely confident. Inside, I had lost every ounce of self-esteem and all belief in myself. I saw myself as a fat, worthless, unlovable blob.

135

After the initial shock, anger, hurt and fear began to wear off, I turned away from self-pity and started to concentrate on my kids. I was determined to pull it together to give them some semblance of a normal, loving life. To do that, however, I realized that I had to start taking care of myself.

I joined a gym and Weight Watchers™ and lost 25 pounds. I worked on getting out of debt. Eventually, I reached out to women friends and "asked" for help. I read every self-help book available. I had to figure out my part in the divorce and take responsibility for my own actions. I worked and worked on forgiveness. I started on a path towards spirituality, really questioning my own belief in God, and discovering my true purpose.

Where was this new path leading? Well, I had been a family law attorney for about 10 years at the time of my divorce. I wanted to empower my clients to take charge of their lives, not just to "win" their cases. But it wasn't until I personally went through a divorce myself that I really understood the pain and transformation of divorce. I am a much better divorce attorney-mediator as a result of my own experience.

Three years after my divorce, I went to a "Body and Soul" conference sponsored by Omega Institute. I went to a workshop with Cheryl Richardson, who is a "life coach." I was so thrilled and motivated by her talk that I hired my own coach. At this point, I was newly remarried. I credit my coach with saving my current marriage, as I was clearly bringing into it my fears and distrust from the previous one. At the end of one year, I knew I needed to become a coach and share what I learned with other people going through difficult life transitions.

Since graduating from coaching school, I have been leading life makeover classes for the local community college, and coaching private individuals. I created another class called "Transcend through Divorce" and began writing a book. I have had the honor of attending many workshops and learning from the man who I consider the greatest life coach of our time, Anthony Robbins. I am traveling (living my dreams) on a regular basis and as an attorney and life coach, I get to work with hundreds of people every single year as they "Transcend" through their situations.

I am passionately carrying the message that divorce is not a tragedy! It often is a blessing in disguise and, for me, it is a gift to witness so many other people blossom into the persons they were meant to be.

I thank God my ex-husband did what he did, and I thank him for freeing me to step into the extra-ordinary life I was meant to lead!

Lori Rubenstein
Attorney and Life Coach
1032 SE Lane Avenue
Roseburg, OR 97470
541-673-6901
lori@attorney-coach.com
www.daretotranscend.com

The Answer to a Prayer
Warren Whitlock

There I was: working in my chosen profession, making a living and raising a family. But I dreamed of being an entrepreneur, so I bought real estate and made more money each year.

Then suddenly, my job ended. I found a new job within two days, but that company sold after six months. I switched again. A few months later, I found myself out of a job for the third time in eleven months. My property was in escrow and a buyer had backed out, leaving the units damaged. I was in debt, out of work, and needed desperately to unload my rentals. Then I woke up.

I knew I had to start my own business, but I had no idea WHAT business. No one I knew had advice for me. So I turned to prayer. I hoped God would help me pay the bills. Next morning, I got a phone call from a real estate prospect I was working with the week before. She needed someone to come in and consult on a project. There'd be a lot of work, and I would be busy indefinitely. Within 24 hours, I had a large check deposited in my first business account and went to work on the first of many consulting jobs.

Some time later, I asked my first client why she called me. She told me that she felt overwhelmed with work, but suddenly felt that she should call me to get help -- at the same time I was praying for help. I'm convinced that I received divine help when I needed it; help that came after I decided what I needed to do. The help was an opportunity, not a handout.

Later, I found that there was no one refilling toner cartridges for my laser printer, so looked into a business opportunity. The first system I looked at was disappointing, but a cassette tape with the presentation was playing when my father visited my office. He listened, liked the idea, and next thing we knew, we were in a businesses. I was not just making a living; I was employing my dad!

15 years later, I still sell toner cartridges, and our printer service

137

has mushroomed into a nationwide sales business. I do what I love to do every day. offering free printer tech support at and writing web copy that sells my products.

No matter what your situation, you can choose to live your life as you want. Work at it, and powers beyond your comprehension will come to your aid.

Warren Whitlock, HeadSpinner
www.landmarkprinters.com
www.laserpage.com

138

LIVE THE LIFE YOU LOVE

The Top 7 Secrets to Small Business Success
As learned from my twin 3 year-olds
Troy White

Small business success is very similar to learning to walk, talk and spell. The basics have to be understood before moving on to the next step. I am blessed to have twin 3-year-old girls in my life and I am amazed how much I learn from them every day. I find myself realizing just how well my observations apply to being successful and happy in life and in business.

Take heart in these tips—they may come from little people but they have the power of giants.

- No matter how small you are you can change lots of lives—your goal for starting your business should be to change lives in some way. Remember this in everything you do. Ask, "How can I change my clients' lives?"
- Run naked every once in a while. Well, you don't have to be naked, but run! Have fun, be free and try to be a kid again. Having kids gives you that chance and it's incredible to relive the fun you used to have when you weren't so serious about life and business.
- Climb that wall, no matter how big the wall is. Persistence pays off in the end. Never give up on your dreams and keep on trying.
- The times when you appear small and frail are when you can surprise everyone with your hidden strengths. Most people pay attention to what the big boys are doing and how they became successful. They miss the small businesses that quietly make substantial profits every year. These companies go about their business drawing attention from their clients - not the competition.
- Act like a silly goof whenever and wherever you want—people will never forget you, and that is what every

For your free gift, go to: **www.wakeupand.com**

business owner dreams of: sticking in everyone's mind.

❤ Remember to share. People can get very protective of what they learn and how they achieve success. When you have something of value that would benefit others, share! It will come back to you one hundred fold.

❤ Lie back on the grass and watch the clouds go by whenever you have a chance. Reflection and relaxation can be the most powerful combination that you have in your personal and business success—use it!

To your happiness and success!

Troy White
www.SmallBusinessCopywriter.com.
Helping entrepreneurs jump start their business success and profit growth
through uncommon, yet highly profitable, marketing techniques.
troy@smallbusinesscopywriter.com

140

Quality Ingredients Yield A Quality Life
Glen Bickerstaff

"In all things, seek quality."
"Always take the high road"
"Character is defined by what one does when no one else is looking."

We live by simple rules and yet these rules can be very challenging. We are constantly faced with choices that try to divert our attention from the "high road," challenge our commitment to quality over quantity, and test our characters. Our response to these situations defines us to others but more importantly, to ourselves. The rewards of following the rules are often subtle but very valuable. Knowing we have the ability to overcome daily challenges promotes our self-confidence, self-esteem, a sense of responsibility, and stature among our peers. In dealing with any situation, it is important to keep the following in mind: If you want to be liked, be likeable. If you want to be admired, be admirable. If you want to be trusted, be trustworthy.

141

Surround yourself with people of high moral character. Watch them. See how they respond to the challenges they face. Encourage them to "do the right thing." Model your own behavior after those people and heed your own advice and encouragement. Be generous to others and give freely of yourself. Ask nothing in return. These "gifts" will come back to you especially in the quality of people you attract and the quality of friendships you make. Throughout life, nothing will provide greater enjoyment and satisfaction.

Act with integrity. See the big picture and understand the value of long-term vision. The quality of your life will not be based on short-term gratification gained at the expense of compromised values. A victory that requires a journey outside of one's ethical boundaries will tarnish quickly and ring hollow upon reflection.

A victory from fair and ethical competition will bring a lifelong enjoyment. Embrace the fatigue that comes from honest and complete effort. Bask in the simple satisfaction of doing your best and knowing that you have earned the fruits of your labors.

Finally, be strong. Have the courage to stand for what is right and follow through with your actions. Be willing to make the choices that maintain your position on the high road and emphasize high quality, long-term outcomes. Follow the simple rules and you will have the finest experiences one can have.

Glen Bickerstaff
#1 Money Manager, U.S.
Front Page, Money Magazine (Sept. 2001)

142

The Happier You Are, The Happier You Are
Jennifer Hough

Have you ever noticed that the happier you are,
the happier you are?

For example, take my dog, Zack. His intention is to show his love for me by protecting me from those (as he perceives) nasty neighbors passing by outside. He proudly prances back to my desk looking at me knowing that I love him for his brave growl, and will hug him for his bravery. He does what makes him feel good and that includes getting snuggled, protecting me, going for walks, eating—he is quite a genius actually. He has the ability to know what he loves to do, to do it, and be present for the self-appreciation and (if you are fortunate) the appreciation of others. Here is the other skill that Zack has mastered; he has the ability to take his attention off things that make him feel bad, and put them onto things that make him feel good. For example; let's say he is hungry and it is a miserable feeling. So he barks for about 30 seconds and then decides that is not worth the anguish and proceeds to hunt squirrels outside. How long do we spend nagging for things for which the timing is not right? Why not focus on something that feels good, and trust the process?

Someone once said to me "Jennifer, you are going to be worm-food one day." Though humorous, that is a harsh reality. Why spend your days harping on things that, in the grand scheme of things, are of little importance? Zack doesn't, so what gives me the right to waste away my life on frivolous things?

I have made it my mission in life to minimize the amount of time that I stay in a bad "headspace." It has almost become a contest to see how little time I spend on stuff that "irks" me. My mission in life is to deliberately look for the bright side. Certain things, like getting creatively blocked, a disagreement with my hubby, or Zack scratching the pine floors used to keep me unhappy for weeks. I now have my discontent down to minutes (sometimes hours). Why?

143

First of all, this is the only life I have in this body. I refuse to waste precious time stressing about things that I know will be resolved. Why in God's green acres would I waste time on things that don't feel good, when I have an inner knowing that everything turns out exactly in perfect order?

As a holistic health coach, a keynote speaker and corporate facilitator on "Getting Out of Your Way (and Deliberately Creating What you Want the Easy Way)," I am forced to practice what I preach. Isn't it wonderful that by focusing on things that work, not only do you manifest more success, health, and energy, but you also have the ability to appreciate all of those things?

Zack (the genius dog) is an expert at getting out of his way, deliberately creating a life of joy, and allowing in all the manifestations of his wonderful way of thinking.

We could all learn a lot from Zack.

144

Jennifer Hough CNC HBA CPT
Keynote Speaker *Getting Out of Your Way*
Holistic Lifestyle Coach
Author
www.thevitalyou.com
1-888-669-9744

A Blessed Woman
Nicki Keohohou

I am a blessed woman. Not because of material wealth or notoriety, but because I have had the good fortune to live and work in the presence of people who are acting upon their deepest desires to make a difference. When you surround yourself with purposeful people, it changes you at the very core of your being and inspires you to greatness. So at the age of 52, I found myself with a burning desire to redesign my life and create something so significant that it would forever change my family as well as the industry in which I have worked for 25 years. My desire to make a difference became my calling, and inspired me to take the first steps of what has become the adventure of my life.

The journey began one night while talking with my husband Saf, who is the love of my life. As we shared our dreams for our future it became apparent that I was so busy making a living that I was not living the life I desired. We knew we had to make a change. That night we crafted our future, writing pages and pages of thoughts and desires. We *WANTED IT ALL* and were no longer willing to settle for anything less and promised to do what ever it took to make the dream a reality.

Our ultimate dream included being with our children and grandchildren who lived half way around the world in Hawaii. We wanted to experience the everyday miracles that bond a family together and made the decision to give up the sprawling home in Dallas, pack up our lives, and move.

My vision also included making a difference within the industry I had grown to love—direct selling. I was no longer satisfied to merely "participate," and had a burning desire to create something of such value that it would forever change the future of the profession. This would require that I leave the security of my consulting work and engage the help of two women, my daughter

For your free gift, go to: **www.wakeupand.com**

and a dear friend, to birth what is now the Direct Selling Women's Association. This organization, dedicated to uplifting direct selling women throughout the world, is now touching lives in more than 25 countries and 200 companies, helping them grow, succeed and live the life they love.

Has it been an easy journey since Saf and I redesigned our destiny? Absolutely not! The sacrifices and challenges I've faced have required more from me than I ever thought I had to give. But the rewards are immeasurable. The privilege of seeing my grandson take his first steps, hear my granddaughter's first words and work side by side with my daughter have forever changed my life. And the satisfaction of knowing our work is helping to grow and shift an industry I love has enriched my life beyond my wildest dreams.

Living the life you love requires hard work, a willingness to take risk, an unshakable belief in your dream. Make the decision that today is the day you will take the first step to start living the life of your dreams. The rewards waiting for you on the other side are far greater than any sacrifice you will be asked to make.

Nicki Keohohou
CEO and Co-Founder of the DSWA
nicki@mydswa.org
www.mydswa.org
111 Hekili St., Suite A139
Kailua, HI 96734

Living the Life I Love
Lynn Terry

As a self-employed single mother, I have the best of both worlds: a rewarding career and a flexible schedule that allows me to spend quality time with my children. I truly enjoy my work, and the reward is immeasurable compared to the '9 to 5' job I left seven years ago.

I remember it well: the frustration of commuting to work all week, dropping off and picking up children, and coming home tired only to cook and clean for the family. The house was rented, the car was always breaking down, and there never seemed to be enough money to pay all of the bills.

I felt sure there must be more to life than this, and was determined to find a way to break out of that cycle. That thought took root and blossomed into a plan, and from that point forward I set out to do whatever it would take to turn my dreams into reality.

147

Once you decide to change your life; once your truly believe that you can do anything you set your mind to, your eyes will be open to new ideas and opportunities you were unaware of before. For me, this meant quitting my job to start my first business, and later starting a second business. I had no capital, no assets and no credit. But I had faith in myself, and I was determined to succeed.

Being a business owner is not for everyone, and making a decent income just isn't enough. You really must listen to that little voice in the back of your mind that is ever trying to guide you in the right direction. Whatever you want to do, think you should do, enjoy doing the most -- that is the one thing that will bring you fulfillment in your life. Follow your dreams, because *if you can dream it, you can do it.* This I know.

I wake up every day to a career that I enjoy, two beautiful children, and a lifestyle that I deliberately chose and created for myself. I often wonder how things would have turned out if I hadn't

LIVE THE LIFE YOU LOVE

made that decision. The benefits to my children, and to myself as a woman have been incredible. Along with true happiness came the confidence, pride, independence and a feeling of self-worth that I gained through all of the sacrifices I made to achieve my goals.

Whatever your dream is, I encourage you to make it a reality.

Living the life I love,

Lynn Terry
McMinnville, TN
www.SelfStartersWeeklyTips.com

148

The Most Powerful Thing In Life
Daniel Bushnell

Have you ever asked yourself the question, "What is the single most powerful thing I could be doing with my life?" Answering this question often requires us to dig deep into our souls. In my experience, finding the answer becomes our "greatest juice," our real contribution, that which fuels our life with lasting passion.

My dream had always been to become a filmmaker, to touch people's lives with the power of music and visual effects. Despite my dream, there seemed to be many obstacles in my way. I had neither the background nor the money, and even wondered if I had the talent.

I never gave up on this vision but held it quietly in my heart, like a seed waiting to be germinated one day. Years passed. I went to work in network marketing and generated a strong residual income. Then came the weekend film classes. My "one day" came when I met someone who had made a feature film for less than 3 months salary. At that moment, a light turned on inside. I was convinced that I could do this.

149

For the next two years I lived a life of passion – I was so ON FIRE! I was filled with joy and the creative juices were flooding through as each piece was added to this movie. I could sense that a larger purpose was developing through me. It was like giving birth each day to something that was giving me life!

Of course, the obstacles grew as well. Because of my inexperience, we had to shoot the movie three times before finally getting it right. Money was a constant challenge, the movie became very costly. My sweet and brilliant fiancée even pitched in her resources to help me.

We struggled much, slept little and went into debt. Yet the sheer joy of this project made us immune to anything because it was feeding us on a deeper level. We loved this movie! At the first public screening, we sat in the back just watching people as they broke into laughter and then tears. When they rose for a standing ovation, there was an infinite stream of joy that ran through both of us.

Joseph Campbell said *"follow your bliss."* When we choose to fulfill our purpose, when the light of the soul inspires our daily thoughts and actions, our life becomes one of passion, contribution and deep fulfillment.

Daniel Bushnell
WWW.LIVINGYOUNG.NET
LivingYoung@Earthlink.net

150

Emotional Fitness Starts with Time and Talk
Dr. Barton Goldsmith

In our state (sometimes called the State of Confusion) a lot of time and energy is spent making our bodies fit. There are health clubs and nutrition stores on every block. Many people resort to all kinds of bizarre diets, supplements and even medication to lose weight. They try to change their lifestyles to attain physical health and buy exercises books and videos as if they were treasure maps.

Most people put more time and energy into their hair than their relationships. If we would spend one-tenth the time we take caring for our bodies and put it into our relationships, we would be much happier people and the divorce rate would drop substantially.

The real reason why some relationships work and others fail is that the couples in those working relationships WORK on them. They do this in a variety of ways including sharing feelings, reading and counseling. But all successful relationships have one thing in common: communication.

151

Physical exercise becomes easier the more we do it. Emotional fitness works the same way. Start slowly, perhaps by talking to your partner about one issue that you want to work on. Next you may want to buy a book (or read one), take a workshop, or just take a walk and hold hands. Or you could just experiment with different ways to connect. Pass notes during TV commercials; anything can work. The point is that the more you do it the easier and more comfortable it will be.

Perhaps the most difficult part about achieving emotional fitness in a relationship is determining exactly what to do, or what to talk about in order to get there. It's actually very simple: start with what's in your face at the moment or, as Glinda, the Good Witch of the North, said to Dorothy when she was about to journey down the yellow brick road, *"It's always best to start at the beginning."*

After you've experienced a little success with some communication or emotional exercise, doing it again will be less intimidating. Before you know it you'll actually start to enjoy the process. A number of couples I know actually take the time to talk about their relationships during evening walks or even while bike riding. This casual approach can work well because you release your emotional anxiety through the physical exercise. Once you feel comfortable talking about "emotional stuff" it will be easier to do it the next time and the next.

Just like exercise, getting your relationship emotionally fit requires doing something to get it in shape on a regular basis. Unlike physically working out, staying emotionally fit usually only takes an hour or two a week and a change here or there. That's not much of an investment when you consider the value of the results.

So put down the remote control, let the weeds in your garden grow for an extra hour or so and send the kids to a movie so the two of you can be alone. Once you feel how much happier you become by getting your relationship in shape, you will actually look forward to doing what it takes to achieve emotional fitness.

Dr. Barton Goldsmith, Ph.D.
www.EmotionalFitness.net

A Mission To Love
Mafé Rabino

I am very grateful to God for giving me a loving heart.

I do not have a perfect life; my heart had been broken several times as a result of my parents' separation and from separations in my own relationships. However, as I look back to my experiences, all I have is gratitude in my heart for all the blessings God has bestowed on me. For, in addition to the not-so-happy relationships that taught me great lessons in life, I have enjoyed great friendships and wonderful relationships. Through my experiences, I grew in faith, wisdom and spirit that made me become sensitive to other people's feelings and sentiments.

153

I had a chance to be involved in a group home facility that takes care of the elderly. I thought I was there to give my love to the residents. I thought, because I was younger, that I should serve them. They have served me more than I have served them.

One day I was speaking to one of the residents; an elderly man who was obviously feeling blue. He had said, "Honey, I am not feeling well." I had asked him "Why Papa?" He said "Because I cannot walk. My foot doesn't work." I said, "Do you know Papa that we love you here? That we care for you?" He held my hands and looked into in my eyes. "Honey, I know," he said. Tears rolled down my cheeks. I thought I was just doing a job. I didn't realize that God had sent me on a Mission to Love. Then Papa turned to me and said, "How are you doing, Honey?" I responded "Papa I have a broken heart." He hugged me and said, "I'm sorry, Honey," as if my feelings mattered more than his own troubles.

The following day he saw me again. Out of the blue he asked, "Honey, how is your heart?" I laughed! I was amazed that he remembered what I said the day before because he had dementia. "Papa," I said, "You mended my broken heart."

I thought I had entered an arrangement where I could simply

set up a system. I thought I was there to do something for others. I thought I had a well-defined mission. I was wrong. The residents, too, were living a mission. They had touched my life, my heart and my spirit. Human spirit and human emotion were facets of this business that no management expert could reduce to a mere system.

Human spirit is so powerful. It doesn't age; it cannot be defined by shape, form or color. It is free. When it is challenged it proves itself. When it is inspired it can't help but reveal itself.

Unconditional Love makes us whole and healed, and most of all it, nurtures our human spirit.

Mafé Rabino
Vice President
Synchronized Strategies, Inc.
syncstrategies@aol.com
rabinoassociates@aol.com
(702) 400-4255

154

Six Simple Steps to Success
Jay Aaron

Success can be measured by money, service to others, or simply by how you feel. Achieving success is much easier than you think. Write down the following information according to these—

Six simple steps:

1. Everything you are passionate about. Everything. Morals. Principles. Food. People. Animals. Activities. Dreams and desires. What you love about the world. Write down what you believe you must change.

2. Your life's purpose, your "reason for being." It's big and lofty, yet easily achieved. "My purpose is to love and be loved," for example.

3. Your current life's mission - a specific aim or task that you believe it's your duty to carry out, or is of special importance. "I'm on a mission to clean up my neighbor hood "… to end homelessness." "… to help cure cancer."

4. Your vision. Imagine the world seven generations from now. How would it look, feel, smell? How would people act, and interact?

Choose:

5. One simple action or activity involving something from your "passions" list that you can do to fulfill some or all of your mission. For example, if your mission is to save the whales and you are passionate about eating ice cream, sponsor a fund-raising ice-cream social.

▼

For your free gift, go to: **www.wakeupand.com**

Do:

6. That thing, empowered by a sense of your personal purpose, and knowing that what you do is contributing in some large or small way to creating the world you envision.

Success!

Jay Aaron, M.A.
Author, speaker, consultant and coach
C.E.O. of Aaron Enterprises
www.jayaaron.com
wakeup@jayaaron.com

156

Identifying Identity
Linnea Peery

What are you? Where are you from?
Where are your parents from?

These questions, asked of me since childhood, are some of the ways people have attempted to discern my ethnic heritage. Why did so many need this particular bit of information about me before they sought any deeper knowledge of who I was?

Thus, I have been compelled to think about race, identity and their relationship to one another. To what degree should we human beings identify ourselves with our ethnic heritage?

Nichiren Buddhism's practice of chanting *Nam-myoho-renge-kyo* and learning its philosophy has helped illuminate my questions in this area. Three concepts in particular have been helpful, and one is the concept of eternal life. Buddhism teaches that we continue in a cycle of birth, death and rebirth, bringing with us only the karma we have accumulated in lives before. Nichiren says, "To clearly perceive life and death as the essence of eternal life is realization, or total enlightenment."

This means that I have not necessarily always been female, or bi-racial, or even human. So these traits, as well as others that seem to define my life experience, are transient. The only constant is the Mystic Law of the universe and the cycle of life. So, is race, in its impermanence, to be ignored?

This raises the second Buddhist concept: Mission. According to Buddhism, everything I bring to the table; my strengths, my weaknesses, my hardships and triumphs; becomes fuel for my mission as a Bodhisattva of the Earth, one who seeks to be enlightened and relieve the suffering of others. Nichiren Buddhist teacher Daisaku Ikeda says: "Every person has a singular mission, his or her individuality and way of life. That is the natural order of things."

157

So race matters — and it doesn't.

It matters because it is part of what forms my experience in this lifetime, and therefore, influences my mission. For example, feeling marginalized enables me to feel empathy with others who feel marginalized, thereby contributing to my compassion and ability to help.

Yet Buddhist teachings reveal that humanity's true identity is to be found beneath the surface. The Lotus Sutra, the starting point of Nichiren Buddhism, contains the analogy of two bundles of reeds to illustrate the third Buddhist concept, dependent origination: the interdependence of all living things." These bundles can only stand if they have one another to lean on; neither can exist independently of the other.

It is wonderful to celebrate our heritage, be it cultural, ethnic or spiritual. It is also vital to respect those things in others. But dependent origination teaches that acknowledging only our differences while ignoring the common source of life that connects us all, leads to divisiveness where there should be harmony.

Perhaps, when someone asks me about my background, they are trying to categorize me, or perhaps they are merely curious. Either way, I am confident that my ethnicity, like all my present circumstances, is part of how I uniquely express my true identity as a *Bodhisattva of the Earth* and part of the human family.

Linnea Peery
mystic21st@yahoo.com

For your free gift, go to: **www.wakeupand.com**

A Life of Passion
Joe Antrim

PASSION! It's what separates the men from the boys, the great from the mediocre and the elite from the average. Passion is the fuel of greatness. No one ever achieved anything without passion. It is the inferno of intense desire to succeed that drives one to action.

Lance Armstrong, cancer survivor and five-time winner of the Tour de France, is passion personified. It was reported that one day in December, after his 3rd Tour de France win, he received a call on his cell phone from friend and competitor David Millar. Millar asked, "Tell me you're not on your bike", to which Armstrong replied, "I'm on my bike." Millar yelled back, "it's December bloody first! How long have you been on it?" Armstrong replied, "three and a half hours." Millar screamed! That's passion. Lance Armstrong is the best at what he does because passion is what drives him. He trains harder, longer and smarter than any other cyclist.

Passion gives us power to persuade, perform, and persevere.

Persuade. Without passion, we have no ability to convey thoughts or ideas. Imagine a salesperson without passion for his product or a politician with no passion for his cause. They are ineffective.

Perform. Without passion, when things get tough, we give up. Passion gives us the power to perform regardless of the circumstances around us. We push through the muck and mire and obstacles to attain the goal.

Persevere. In the same way that passion allows us to perform, it helps us persevere. Success is not an overnight process. Like running a marathon, it takes time and patience even when the end is nowhere in sight. Perseverance takes us to the finish.

What drives you? Only you can answer that question. Passion

159

cannot be learned or transferred. It's something that must be brought up from deep within. It's like a buried treasure hidden in the soul. We must seek it, pursue it and dig it up. Unlike gold or jewels, it cannot be plundered nor lose its value. It is with us always and, like a spring when tapped, will provide an endless supply of refreshment and purpose.

What inspires you and makes you a better human being? It's time to look deep within and tap into that never-ending well of passion.

Joe Antrim
Licensed Massage Therapist
Whole Health Massage and Wellness, Inc.
www.whole-health-massage.com

160

Training for your MIND!
Sean Greeley

As a personal trainer, I've found the battle to get in shape is won in the largest muscle of all—your brain. Working out is not "rocket science." Today, everyone has unlimited sources of knowledge on strength training, nutrition, supplementation, flexibility, and cardiovascular exercise. So, it's not hard to learn what you should be doing. The challenge lies in getting it done.

What goes on between your ears makes all the difference.

Recognize that you have the power to think your way around or through any obstacle; employ "teamwork."

I've heard every excuse in the book for failing to reach fitness goals. Some of them are legitimate; some are not: "I'm working two jobs," "I've got two kids," "I don't have the money," "I don't have the time." But whatever obstacles you're facing, they are not unique. Someone, somewhere has faced the same challenges and has found a way to overcome them. You have the power to get it done!

161

I trained a truck driver who was on a schedule of 5 hours driving, 5 hours of sleep. He was home once a week for 24hours— if he was lucky. How could he do his essential cardio work? He figured out that, if he stopped the truck 2 miles before a weigh station, his partner could let him out, and he could walk to the weigh station. He exercised without interfering with his work schedule! He thought his way around his obstacles, used teamwork, and he was able to get it done!

Focus on your positive thoughts and successes and watch them grow!

Negativity is something we all have to guard against: the voices that say "You can't do it," or "It's too hard." Instead of the negative self-talk, focus on the positives. What have you achieved today that takes you one step closer to your goal? Focus on the successes, and watch them grow.

I've watched clients build on small steps and become unstoppable. One woman could barely walk 15 minutes without becoming winded her first day. She focused on adding just 1 minute a day for a month, and today she regularly walks an hour as part of her routine and makes it look easy!

Recognize that Health Requires Balance.

I've worked with several clients who were "stressed-out-workaholics." In the corporate world, they learned better results require that they work harder. So, if they didn't lift more, or go faster, they weren't improving. I help them recognize that improvement comes from balance; balance between exercise, nutrition, and the mind; balance between exercise and recovery.

Use your mind! Recognize the need for balance, recognize that you can think your way around any obstacle, employ team work, and build your success on positive foundations. Your dreams become your realities!

162

Sean Greeley
Certified Personal Trainer with the American Council on Exercise
Orlando, FL.
www.ptbysean.com.

Your Foundation is Showing
Lee Beard

I love this book title: *Wake Up…Life the Life You Love.* If there is anything that I've desired to do in this life, it is to enjoy every day. In this book and in life, you will read and hear lots of words of advice. I want to give you my opinion. Keep in mind it's just an opinion, but it has served me well so far.

The most important thing that I have found in life is the need for a solid foundation. You will find plenty of advice on all manner of subjects. I've found that the best advice is to filter everything through a solid belief foundation, then you will know what fits in your life and what will be beneficial now and in the many years to come. In other words, you should ask, "What is wisdom and truth for me?"

My foundation has been a God who IS love. Not a God who tries to love when the mood strikes but a God who is and can only be and do love. A God who loves me more than I love myself and wants the best for me more than I know how to want it for me; a God who has held on to me when I had given up. I don't begin to understand this kind of love, but I have experienced it none the less. I would stake my life and existence on it.

Almost anyone with whom you talk would say that he wants to be healthy, wealthy and wise. I've come to believe that I want to be wise, healthy and wealthy. Wisdom helps you to know the advice that is appropriate for your life and what mentor or what instruction will take you on the proper path.

The interesting thing about your foundation is that it doesn't show at first. Often, not until the storms come into your life, does the foundation seem to be very important. But you will know if

163

your bedrock belief is solid and others will know if you have chosen wisely that foundation on which you built your family and your fortune.

Lee Beard
Executive Producer
www.cpmkt.com
www.leebeard.com

164

Winter Never Fails To Turn To Spring
Lenore Palmer

Thirty years ago, I embarked on a career as a registered nurse with a burning desire to understand human suffering. Why do human beings suffer? How do we overcome suffering? My quest brought me face to face with my own suffering, which led me to explore creative arts therapies. While studying music therapy, a friend introduced me to a Buddhist chant, "Nam Myo Ho Renge Kyo," the centerpiece of a philosophy which elucidates the law of causality as it exists in human life. I learned that the present, with all of its positive and negative effects, is a result of thoughts, words, and actions (causes) made in the past. This led to my understanding that causes made in the present, create future effects. In studying the philosophy more deeply, I came upon the hopeful phrase, "Winter never fails to turn to spring," the idea that no matter what our past or present sufferings, we can inevitably realize "Spring."

165

Ten years ago, as I confronted my failing marriage, poor health, and the lowest imaginable self esteem, I decided to "walk the walk" of this philosophy. My deepest thoughts, my conscious intention, my strongest determination, my morning and evening prayer became: "To cherish my life and to help others to cherish their lives through art, music, writing, and movement." My first children's book, *"Winter Never Fails to Turn to Spring,"* was born from this determined prayer.

When I showed my book to my therapist, she wept. When I shared the book with the principal of the Montessori school where I worked as an enrichment specialist, she wept. When I presented the book to the Director of Nursing in the hospital where I worked, she paid me to share it with her son's preschool as a gift to his class. My life opened up! I began sharing "Winter Never Fails to Turn to Spring" with psychiatric patients, geriatric patients, with human beings struggling to overcome chemical dependency. In the past nine years, nine more books have grown out of the one phrase, "winter never fails to turn to spring," the spirit to never give up, to muster courage in the face of great difficulties. Every time someone is encouraged with one of my books, I feel my prayer has been answered and my heart is filled with joy.

This joy, I believe, has contributed to the fact that now I am *living the life I love.*

Lenore Palmer
Nurse, Author, Artist, Speaker
www.FlipTales.com

166

To Change Your Life, Change Your Patterns
Rose Martin

When you are aiming at a goal, a target, or a destination—some kind of mark that says, *"This is where I want to be,"* everything you do has to be weighed against the fulfillment of that goal. You must ask yourself, "Will this bring me closer to fulfilling it, take me further away, or make no difference?"

Many times we make the mistake of lumping too many of our decisions into the "makes no difference" category. Then we wonder why we aren't getting closer to our goal, or why it still seems so far away. If we examined the items in the "makes no difference" category, we would see that most of them should have been placed under "takes me further away."

You see, everything makes a difference. There are no thoughts, words, or actions that are "neutral." Each one either falls into the "closer to" or "further away" category. In order for your goal to become a reality, you must change your life patterns so they align with your goal. Evaluate everything you do to determine if it is something that will bring you closer to or move you further away from your goal.

Change the pattern of everything that is not bringing you closer. Put your goal in the forefront of your mind every second, every minute, of every day and then line up everything you do up with it. Don't slack off! Continue to develop the life pattern that will lead to the fulfillment of your goal. The more decisions you make that fall in line with your goal, the closer you will be to reaching it.

In order to change your life and the results you are getting, you must consciously do things differently. And you must do them differently day after day, month after month, and year after year. Realize that everything you do matters. Change your life patterns so

167

the things you think, say, and do line up with where you want to be. When your thoughts, words, and actions fall into the "bring me closer to" category your goals will become reality!

Rose Martin
Author: *Eternal Life Skills*
Perfect Will Ministries, Inc.
1920-117 Centerville Tnpk., #346
Virginia Beach, VA 23464
757.474.7955
rose@perfectwill.com
www.perfectwill.com

168

Your Lows Create Your Highs!
Scott Schilling

Adversity sucks—until you realize it has an incredible ability to force you to grow. Fortunately, I've had a number of negative events in my life. I say "fortunate" because, while recovering, I was forced to look inside and grow my very being.

I played Big 10 football, starting as a sophomore. I was pretty good; "Destined for the NFL," some said. The "Big Head" set in along with my successes. Simply put, I became a jerk.

It was two weeks into the '77 season and we were about to play our cross-state rival on national TV. All week I heard, "You're going to win it for us." I needed to unwind from the pressures, so I decided to play golf with a buddy. Between the 12th green and 13th tee box, our golf cart began to flip, throwing me out. It landed on my kicking foot, completely severing my Achilles tendon. In a flash, I was out for the season. Worse: I was told my injury would end my career and my ability to participate in sports of any kind. What a way to gain back some humility quickly!

Ultimately, I came back to play football again in college, win nine club racqetball championships and became a scratch golfer—all things that people suggested I'd never be able to accomplish.

Years later, I got married, grew my career, and had two beautiful children. Then, my marriage dissolved. I turned to a counselor to help me understand what I needed to do to grow myself appropriately. Previously, I would have never searched out that guidance. It caused me to regain my passion and enthusiasm for learning.

Today, my son Taylor is Number 5 in his junior class, a two-sport athlete and gives 300 hours a year to community service! My daughter Jordan is ranked high in her class, plays three sports and donates her time at church. They are both incredible!

My wife of nearly nine years, Peggy, is the most wonderful

169

woman in the universe. We have grown together in ways I never dreamed possible. We have invested in each other far beyond our previous efforts with others. Through adversity, I've learned to cherish my spouse, to grow a wonderful, loving relationship!

While neither event was pleasant, both positively redefined me as a person. Adversity can only keep you down if you let it. Getting knocked down becomes a problem only if you don't get back up and learn from it. Welcome your adversities; opportunity waits on the other side!

Scott Schilling
Swschilling@hotmail.com
www.scottschilling.com

170

The Value of Pleasing Manners
Shannon Smith

An individual's manners are the index of his tastes, feelings, temper and usually indicate true character.

Some people assume a kind of conventionally polite manner; a superficial veneer on special occasions. This "society cloak" is of little importance, of no practical value, and is as transparent as it is worthless. Artificial politeness is an attempt to deceive, an effort to make others believe that we are what we are not.

True politeness is the outward expression of the natural character, the external signs of the internal being. It must be born of sincerity and be the response of the heart, for no amount of "surface polish" can substitute for honesty and truthfulness. A beautiful character is simply a heart filled with honest intentions.

Good manners are developed through a spirit imbued with unselfishness, kindness, justness and generosity. When we realize that they are the outward expression of inward virtues, (like the hands of a watch indicating that the machinery within is perfect and true), we will then understand the power of applying the golden rule.

Unfortunately, we are often compelled to do business with an individual whose very presence makes us uncomfortable; who is devoid of noble qualities. On the other hand, we come in contact with those whose personalities are like the golden rays of a June sun, warming and gentle.

Today, more than ever, the nobler qualities of mind and heart count.

History is crowned with examples illustrating the power of indefinable charm of style. Among the qualities which contribute to worldly success, true politeness takes first rank. It is the bearing of man towards his fellowman, more than any other circumstance that promotes or obstructs his advancement of success in life. We court and seek the friendship of an individual with genuine character, while shunning the one who is gruff and cold.

For your free gift, go to: **www.wakeupand.com**

171

LIVE THE LIFE YOU LOVE

Pleasing manners constitute one of the golden keys that open the door leading to success and happiness. Good manners are simply the crowning jewel of a noble character. The great motivating power of our conduct is the heart; it is the foundation of all action.

WHEN THE HEART IS RIGHT, LIFE WILL BE RIGHT!

Shannon Smith
Image Strategist
Author, Speaker, TV personality
Premiere Image International
Toronto, Canada
www.premiereimageintl.com
416.324.8955

172

Infusing the World with the Passion of Spirit
Demi Mazzola

So many people, today, are striving to improve their lives by restoring health and vigor to a body damaged by poor diet, lack of exercise, and neglect. In many cases, they turn first to physical training. They work hard, but, for some reason, they find little improvement.

If you have been training endlessly without achieving the results you desire, remember: training for life-long results is not just about training your body. Your mind and spirit are equally important. A true transformation starts within.

As a fitness trainer, I have witnessed how much a "spiritually deprived" person can suffer, even after accomplishing astounding transformations with the body. I listened with the compassionate heart that drives me and I have been inspired.

I sought something that would assist me with my "spirit training." In addition to exercise, I added an audio program that was uplifting, rejuvenating, and replenishing for the soul. I included guided imagery, positive affirmations, and subliminal-like messages that talk to the spirit.

There is really nothing like it. If you live anywhere in the San Fernando Valley, I can share this with you. The first "Spirit Slide Studios" opened its doors on November 1, 2003. I am working to bring it to everyone's neighborhood.

For the present, I am thrilled to tell Californians "If you would like to escape from your everyday routine, escape to Spirit Slide Studios where you will be guided to your private room complete with your very own Spirit Slide™." You can "slide" yourself up and down, like rocking a baby, while listening to this indescribable audio program through cordless headphones. The atmosphere is warm, inviting and very relaxing. Candles flicker in the dim lighting, aromatherapy fills the room that tickles your senses. Trickling water flows from a beautiful fountain to help you escape into nature.

I designed the program to heal, calm, nurture and nourish the spirit, but now I realize that there may be more than toning and physical health at stake. I know the Spirit Slide program will help millions, perhaps those in great stress who are fighting serious disease; perhaps those who are terminally ill and seeking peace.

I pray for the guidance and the wisdom to make it happen with honor, integrity and compassion. I pray for your help, as well, for readers of this book recognize the union of mind, body and spirit. With your help, WE CAN MAKE IT HAPPEN! I hope you will not hesitate to contact me with your thoughts.

Demi Mazzola
Creator of the *Spirit Slide* program
CEO Spirit Slide Studios and
Demi-Lawrence Body Works
Spirit Slide Studios
21516 Victory Blvd.
Woodland Hills, CA 91367
818-713-9922
818-652-7922(cell)
www.demi-lawrence.com
spiritslide@msn.com

174

United We Stand, Divided We Fall
Oliver Nims

The opportunity is upon us, to create a new culture of peace.

The culture of war, as old as humanity itself, has come to a head. It is no longer an acceptable way to solve conflict. The culture of war is sustained by greed, anger and stupidity and is also one of reaction; focusing on the effects rather than the cause. It is as effective as trying to lose weight by drinking diet soda, or paying bills with your credit cards. Silly! The culture of war is full of customs like violence, defense, power struggle, revenge, escalation.

Let's look at another possibility, the culture of peace. While you may say it has never existed, I beg to differ. The culture of peace is evident in friendship, cultural exchanges, diplomacy, and the United Nations. When we travel to other countries, isn't it ironic that we can't help but see more similarities than differences in people? Cultures and religions are different. Language is different but when translated, we're all talking about the same things. Religions have different names for their gods but they're still the same god.

175

It's also interesting that, while the world is in the throes of war, there has never been so much possibility for peace. The infrastructure is in place. Never before have we been so connected through Internet, commerce, and travel with the world. For the first time in history you could be carrying on a long distance relationship with your girlfriend in Katmandu for free via the Internet and, if you really missed her, you could be transported to her doorstep in less than 24 hours for under $1,000.

Where was your car made? Even if it is American, some of its parts were made in other countries. Your whole wardrobe, unless you made it yourself, came from somewhere else.

My point is this, we live in a global village where we are connected, like it or not. This culture of peace will require of us to be aware that we are all sharing this tiny rock flying through space with everyone else. Why not get to know our neighbors. It's never been easier than now!

I have a challenge for you, if you choose to accept it. For the next month try to see a piece of yourself in every person you meet. When you see that thing, even if you don't like it, accept it and respect it. Bless that person and their humanity—appreciate them.

That's good for a start. See how you feel. Banish your fear, talk to strangers. Make friends with immigrants. Try to view the world with a kindly eye. Then once you have that down, go international! Take a trip to an exotic country! Hang out with the locals!

The key is to be open-hearted, and remember,
united we stand, divided we fall.

Oliver Nims,
Salon owner, educator
wakeupbeauty@yahoo.com

176

Embrace Silence
Dr. Wayne Dyer

You live in a noisy world, constantly bombarded with loud music, sirens, construction equipment, jet airplanes, rumbling trucks, leaf blowers, lawn mowers, and tree cutters. These manmade, unnatural sounds invade your sense and keep silence at bay.

In fact, you've been raised in a culture that not only eschews silence, but is terrified of it. The car radio must always be on, and any pause in conversation is a moment of embarrassment that most people quickly fill with chatter. For many, being alone in silence is pure torture.

The famous scientist Blaise Pascal observed, "All man's miseries derive from not being able to sit quietly in a room alone."

The Value of Silence

With practice, you can become aware that there's a momentary silence in the space between your thoughts. In this silent space, you'll find the peace that you crave in your daily life. You'll never know that peace if you have no spaces between your thoughts.

The average person is said to have 60,000 separate thoughts every day. With so many thoughts, there are almost no gaps. If you could reduce that number by half, you would open up an entire world of possibilities for yourself. For it is when you merge in the silence and become one with it that you reconnect to your source and know the peacefulness that some call God. "Be still and know that I am God," says it so beautifully in Psalms of the Old Testament. The key words are "still" and "know."

"Still" actually means silence. Mother Theresa described silence and its relationship to God by saying, "God is the friend of Silence. See how nature (trees, grass) grows in silence; see the stars, the moon and the sun – how they move in silence. We need silence to be able to touch souls." This includes your soul!

It's really the space between the notes that makes the music

177

you enjoy so much. Without the spaces, all you would have is one continuous noisy note. Everything that's created comes out of silence. Your thoughts emerge from the nothingness of silence. Your words come out of this void. Your very essence emerged from emptiness.

Those who will supersede us are waiting in the vast void. All creativity requires some stillness. Your sense of inner peace depends on spending some of your life energy in silence to recharge your batteries, remove tension and anxiety, thus reacquainting you with the joy of knowing God and feeling closer to all of humanity. Silence reduces fatigue and allows you to experience your own creative juices.

The second word in the Old Testament observation, "know," refers to making your personal and conscious contact with God. To know God is to banish doubt and become independent of others' definitions and descriptions of God. Instead, you have your own personal knowing. And, as Melville reminded us so poignantly, "God's one and only voice is silence."

Dr. Wayne Dyer
Author of *Real Magic* and *Manifesting Your Destiny*
www.waynedyer.com

179

Aaron, Jay

Jay Aaron, M.A., author, speaker, consultant and coach
C.E.O. of Aaron Enterprises
www.jayaaron.com
wakeup@jayaaron.com

Allen, Robert G.

#1 New York Times best selling author of *Nothing Down,
Multiple Streams of Income* and *Creating Wealth*
Co-author of *One Minute Millionaire*

Andrews, Mary

Marper12@aol.com

Antion, Tom

tom@antion.com
www.antion.com
www.public-speaking.org

Antrim, Joe

Licensed Massage Therapist
Whole Health Massage and Wellness, Inc.
www.whole-health-massage.com

Athwal, Reg

CEO, RAW LTD, Surrey, England
Author, Speaker, Trainer, Entrpreneur
Co-author *The Inspirational Poet*
www.regathwal.com
ra@regathwal.com

Bacak, Matt

The Powerful Promoter
1-866-MATT-123
Matt@ultraadvance.com
www.powerfulpromoter.com

Beard, Lee

Involvement with international production,
marketing and advertising
Worked with such personalities as Dick Clark, Dolly Parton,
Steve Martin, Lee Ann Womack, Bob Hope, Kenny Rogers,
Lucille Ball, Bee Gees, Mary Tyler Moore, Walter Cronkite.
Lee@businessolympians.com
www.cpmkt.com
www.BusinessOlympians.com
www.leebeard.com

Bella, Rich

Business Owner/ Fitness Expert
866-435-8003
www.rasetraining.com

Bernstein, Mike

mbthebern@aol.com

Bickerstaff, Glen

#1 Money Manager,
U.S. Front Page, Money Magazine (Sept. 2001)

Black, Jackie Ph.D.

California
www.DrJackieBlack.com
DrJackie@DrJackieBlack.com
888-792-6224

Boren, Larry

Broker, L B Brokerage, Inc.
562-708-9878
boren@lbbrokerage.com

Bushnell, Daniel

www.livingyoung.net
livingyoung@earthlink.net

For your free gift, go to: **www.wakeupand.com**

Dyer, Dr. Wayne

Author of *Real Magic and Manifesting Your Destiny*
www.waynedyer.com

Ellermeyer, William K

You Are the Enterprise
Career Coach, Irvine CA
949-786-5490
elosman@aol.com

Fahey, Pamela

Wife, mother, grandmother, entrepreneur
www.truestoriesonline.com
pam@truestoriesonline.com

Ferrigno, Carla

Author of *Women Only: Carla Ferrigno's Total Shape-Up Program*
Over 20 years as certified fitness trainer
Movies: *Black Roses* and *The Seven Magnificent Gladiators*

Fields, Ronald J.

#1 Best Selling Author
Emmy Award Winning Writer
www.wcbiz.com

Figueroa, Eric

Father
Ericfig2000@yahoo.com

Fry, Mike

Entrepreneur
317-299-8900
www.fancyfortunecookies.com

Gibson, Marilyn

1-800-441-8786
www.hangingbyastring.com

Goldsmith, Barton, Ph.D.

www.EmotionalFitness.net

Gospodarek, Dr. Jason

Optometrist, Success Coach, and Author
Jason@InnovativeCoaching.com
www.InnovativeCoaching.com
www.JasonGospodarek.com

Goto, Yasuyuki

American Contact Office
Las Vegas Millionaires, Inc.
Las Vegas, NV
702-279-1712
successjapan@dialogjapan.com
www.yazgoto.com

Greeley, Sean

A.C.E. Certified Personal Trainer
Orlando, FL
1-888-481-5037
www.ptbysean.com

Grosnickle, Lodavina

M.S.T.G Solutions
www.gorgeousludy.us
ludyg2002@yahoo.com

Hansen, Mark Victor

America's Ambassador of Possibility
Newport Beach, CA
Co-author of *Chicken Soup for the Soul* series and
the *One Minute Millionaire.*
Founder of "Goal-Mining Challenge"
www.markvictorhansen.com

Harper, Pamela, RN

Certified Addiction Counselor and
Certified Clinical Hypnotherapist
Writer, Lecturer, Media Personality
Family and Holistic Health • San Clemente, CA.
Pamelaharper@permanentchanges.com

For your free gift, go to: **www.wakeupand.com**

Henderson, R. Winn, M.D

International Radio Talk Show
Host of *Share Your Mission*, Author of 13 Books,
and founder of The Destiny House.
dhenderson7@mchsi.com.
www.theultimatesecrettohappiness.com

Hockings, Dr. Jeff

President/C.E.O.
First Class Marriage
1-800-914-5547
www.FirstClassMarriage.com
drjeffhockings@hotmail.com

Hough, Jennifer CNC HBA CPT

Keynote Speaker "Getting Out of Your Way"
Holistic Lifestyle Coach, Author
1-888-669-9744
www.thevitalyou.com

Hudson, Orrin C.

President, Be Someone, Inc.
770-484-1887
orrin@besomeone.org
www.besomeone.org

Huss, Judge William

Co-author of *Working with Your Homeowners Association;*
A Guide for Living
Author of the forthcoming book *Shake On It;*
Meditating your Way To Success

Keohohou, Nicki

CEO and Co-Founder of the DSWA
Kailua, HI
nicki@mydswa.org.
www.mydswa.org.

Kersey, Cynthia

Nationally-known speaker, columnist
Author of the bestseller, *Unstoppable*
and upcoming sequel *Unstoppable Women*
www.unstoppable.net.

185

For your free gift, go to: **www.wakeupand.com**

Kim, Gil

President and CEO, MSTG Solution
www.mstgs.com

Krawczyk, Richard M. PhD

Author and Lecturer
Author of *Financial Aerobics, Credit Aerobics*
As well as other books and home study courses
www.FinancialFitnessTips.com

Kumar, Dr. Shailendra

Cupertino, CA
408-832-4296

Lamarche, Dr. Gilles

www.gilleslamarche.com
gilles@gilleslamarche.com

Lam, Wing

Founder and Co-Owner, Wahoo's Fish Taco
Wing.lam@wahoos.com

Larner, David

Internet Marketing Expert
818-986-7200
dlarner@tmcla.com
www.tmcla.com

Levine, Michael

Entertainment publicist
Representative for major celebrities ranging from
Barbra Streisand, Michael Jackson, Sandra Bullock,
to Nancy Kerrigan.
Author of 14 books
www.levinepr.com

Levine, Terri

Best-selling Author and Speaker
Author of *Work Yourself Happy, Stop Managing, Start Coaching!,
Coaching For an Extraordinary Life* and *Create Your Ideal Body*
www.coachinginstruction.com
www.terrilevine.com

For your free gift, go to: **www.wakeupand.com**

Lublin, Jill

CEO, Promising Promotions
Author, National Best-Seller *Guerrilla Publicity*
Syndicated Radio Host, *Do The Dream*
415-883-5455
www.promisingpromotion.com
jill@planetlink.com

Marr, Don

Speaker, Author of *A Gateway to Higher Consciousness,*
My Father Calls Me (One Man's Way Back To GOD)
Idealself@aol.com
www.1stbooks.com

Marr, Ryan

Author/ Student
Los Alamitos High School
IdealSelf@aol.com

Martin, Rose

Host of E*ternal Life Skills* radio program,
author of *Eternal Life Skills—*
How to Improve Your Life Today,
While Preparing For Your Future in Heaven
Inspirational Speaker
757-474-7955
rose@eternallifeskills.com
www.eternallifeskills.com

Mazzola, Demi

Creator of the *Spirit Slide* program
CEO *Spirit Slide Studios* and *Demi-Lawrence Body Works*
Woodland Hills, CA
818-713-9922
demified22@msn.com
www.demi-lawrence.com

Mazzullo, Mary E.

Pastor, Photographer, Writer, Entrepreneur
Facilitator of Personal and Financial Growth
mmazzullo@YourFreeAgentPath.com
www.OceanCityWeddings.com
www.YourFreeAgentPath.com

188

For your free gift, go to: **www.wakeupand.com**

Pierce, Lynn

The Sales Therapist
Author, *Getting to YES Without Selling*
480-242-5929
www.changeonething.com

Rabino, Mafé

Vice President, Synchronized Strategies, Inc.
syncstrategies@aol.com
rabinoassociates@ail.com
702-400-4255

Ragland, Pam

President and Founder: Aiming Higher Success Coaching
949-713-7303
www.AimingHigher.com
Pam@AimingHigher.com

Reid, Greg S.

Best selling author, *The Millionaire Mentor*
GregReid@AlwaysGood.com
www.AlwaysGood.com

Rodger, Symeon, Rev. Dr.

Orthodox Church in America
www.symeonrodger.com

Rubenstein, Lori

Attorney and Life Coach
Roseburg, OR
541-673-6901
lori@attorney-coach.com
www.daretotranscend.com

Russell, John

Published Fitness Author
Certified Personal Fitness Trainer
Certified Kickboxing Instructor
john@fittrainer1on1.com
www.fittrainer1on1.com

Schilling, Scott

Swschilling@hotmail.com
www.scottschilling.com

For your free gift, go to: **www.wakeupand.com**

AUTHOR INDEX...

Schmitt, Steven E.
Creator of the *Wake Up...Live the Life You Love series*
Stevene@businessolympians.com
www.businessolympians.com
www.stevene.com

Schmitt, Wendy
Loving Wife of Steven E

Sloan, Clint
World Renowned Artist
www.clintsloan.com

Smartt, Stacey
Founder, Svelte For Life
McDonald, TN
423-432-2195
slsmartt@earthlink.net

Smith, Keith Cameron
Kcs@cfl.rr.com

Smith, Shannon
Image Strategist, Author, Speaker, TV personality
Premiere Image International
Toronto, Canada
416-324-8955
www.premiereimageintl.com

Terry, Lynn
McMinnville, TN
www.SelfStartersWeeklyTips.com

Vitale, Joe
Author of the #1 best-seller, *Spiritual Marketing,
Hypnotic Writing, Adventures Within: Confessions of
an Inner World Journalist,* and the
#1 best-selling audioprogram,
The Power of Outrageous Marketing
www.mrfire.com

For your free gift, go to: **www.wakeupand.com**

WAKE UP... AUTHOR INDEX

White, Troy

troy@smallbusinesscopywriter.com
www.SmallBusinessCopywriter.com

Whitlock, Warren

Head Spinner
www.landmarkprinters.com
www.laserpage.com

Wyland

Artist of the Sea
www.wyland.com

191

For your free gift, go to: **www.wakeupand.com**

WAKE UP... NOTES

192

For your free gift, go to: **www.wakeupand.com**